Jesus
and
Money

Jesus
and
Money

A Guide for Times
of Financial Crisis

Ben Witherington III

Brazos Press
a division of Baker Publishing Group
Grand Rapids, Michigan

© 2010 by Ben Witherington III

Published by Brazos Press
a division of Baker Publishing Group
P.O. Box 6287, Grand Rapids, MI 49516-6287
www.brazospress.com

Printed in the United States of America

Library of Congress Cataloging-in-Publication Data
Witherington, Ben, 1951–
    Jesus and money : a guide for times of financial crisis / Ben Witherington III.
        p. cm.
    Includes bibliographical references and index.
    ISBN 978-1-58743-274-3
    1. Wealth—Biblical teaching. 2. Money—Biblical teaching. 3. Jesus Christ—
Teachings. I. Title.
    BS2545.W37W58 2010
    261.8′5—dc22   2009028631

Unless otherwise noted, scripture translations are the author's own.

10   11   12   13   14   15   16   7   6   5   4   3   2   1

Contents

Abbreviations

1QS	Rule of the Community
AB	Anchor Bible
ABR	*Australian Biblical Review*
b.	Babylonian Talmud
CBQ	*Catholic Biblical Quarterly*
CD	Damascus Document
HUCA	*Hebrew Union College Annual*
JBL	*Journal of Biblical Literature*
Jdt.	Judith
JSNT	*Journal for the Study of the New Testament*
m.	Mishnah
Macc.	Maccabees
NCBC	New Cambridge Bible Commentary
NIBC	New International Biblical Commentary
NIGTC	New International Greek Testament Commentary
NTS	*New Testament Studies*
Q	Qumran
RSV	Revised Standard Version
SEG	Supplementum epigraphicum graecum
Sir.	Sirach
SP	Sacra Pagina
WBC	Word Biblical Commentary
Wis.	Wisdom of Solomon

Prequel

Reconsidering the Value of Money in Hard Times

Why a book on money, and why now? Because our economy is in a free fall. We have worked our way into at least a recession, if not a depression. And all the king's horses and all the king's men won't be able to put Humpty Dumpty back together again—at least not quickly. For at least a while, what lies ahead for most of us is pain and sacrifice, not indulgence and conspicuous consumption. Whether we like it or not (and who does like it?), we now have to learn to live with less. Given the state of the world economy since late 2008, we are not as secure in our trust that the market cannot fail, that there will always be plenty of money at hand. Maybe now is a good time— even a necessary time—to reconsider what money means to us and how we use it (and are used by it), and especially to look anew at what Jesus and his earliest followers really taught about wealth and possessions.

My Southern Baptist granny, who lived through the Great Depression of the 1930s, had an expression for the situation we find ourselves in these days. "We are in a mell of hess," she would say. And since we are in a mess and can't avoid serious cleanup on aisle three for a while, it might be useful to ask ourselves how we got into this "hess." I'll leave the macro-answers on faults in the global economy to economists and politicians. Here, I'll simply focus on the micro-answers of how we *all* have contributed to this problem.

First, most of us are living beyond, and in some cases well beyond, our means. I'm not talking about having a home mortgage or a car payment. I'm talking about paying for almost everything on credit, rather than paying as we go. The rise of the credit card industry in this country in my lifetime, and our love of using the plastic whether it's financially responsible to do so or not, has helped turned the USA into a debtor nation. Never mind that we are also debtors to other world powers like China and oil-producing nations like Saudi Arabia. I'm talking about each of us as individuals abusing credit without hesitation, limitation, or moral reservation. Our spending habits have gotten out of control. And they are frankly quite un-Christian, as we shall see when we revisit the teachings of Jesus and the first Christians.

Second, we have been conditioned to think, even by some preachers in the church, that we are entitled to success, entitled to wealth, entitled to a lifestyle of the rich and famous. In the process, we have muted our consciences when it comes to moral responsibility for what we buy, when we buy it, and how much. And we have learned to spend freely without thinking about our obligations to those less fortunate than ourselves. What the advertisers keep appealing to is that self-centered sense of entitlement.

Further, we have been led to think that we can obtain the ends we want without sacrifice. Gambling in its various forms, including state lotteries, has grown like kudzu over a giant pine forest. And of course the premise behind gambling is that with only a little investment we might strike it big and be set for life. The issue of commensurability of outcome based on input of hard work is not considered. So the gambling culture undermines the old maxim about "an honest day's pay for an honest day's work." The link between work and reward is severed.

Somehow we have arrived at the point of assuming that we must spoil our children. So money we could have spent on necessary things, on charitable giving, or on ministry opportunities is instead spent on luxurious cars and (elective) cosmetic surgery for our children. Basic dictionary definitions of the word *spoil* include "to damage seriously" and "to impair the quality" of those who are spoiled. So we really are not helping our children. And in any event, exorbitant spending for our children feeds the engine of conspicuous consumption and deepens debt.

Entertainment is king, and luxury is desirable. If we were to ask economists what most Americans do with their disposable income, many would tell us that instead of saving money, we spend it on entertainment or luxuries for ourselves. In many cases, we feed our desires before we even meet our needs. Our spending priorities are out of whack. We've supersized our food, our cars, and ourselves.

Even more, the Bible has some pretty stout and stark things to say about believers not lending money at interest to fellow believers. It is a sign of our times that Christians think nothing of charging other people interest, or for that matter paying obscene rates of interest themselves so they may, with credit, buy on demand. We hardly give it a second thought—that is, until the bills come due. I have real sympathy for people who are losing their homes during this economic downturn. But unfortunately many of our wounds are self-inflicted. We buy bigger homes than we can afford, and predatory lenders lick their chops over getting people to sign on the dotted line, even when the persons in question don't really know or understand even basic things like whether the interest rate on their mortgage is fixed or adjustable.

Even when we do save some money, many Christians save it exclusively for their own retirement. I was disgusted the other day to see an RV with a Christian fish symbol on it, and next to it was a bumper sticker that read "I'm spending my grandchildren's inheritance"—as if this were humorous or something to celebrate.

In a culture where the new is the true, and the latest is said to be greatest, Christians get caught up in the fads, trends, and trajectories of frivolous fashion, foolish financial deals, and, in general, indulgence beyond anything healthy, helpful, or holy. All heads are bowed, all eyes are closed—so raise your hand if you or your children are guilty!

I could go on with one illustration after another, but this should suffice to make the point that what determines how most Christians view money, lending, giving, one's economic lifestyle, and a host of related matters is not the Bible, but rather cultural factors and influences.

What's Wrong with This Picture?

Not too long ago I was stuck at an airport in Dallas. On one of those unavoidable airport TV screens, there appeared a televangelist. I won't name names. It could have been any one of a dozen famous purveyors of the prosperity gospel. This one had perfectly coiffed hair, an Armani suit pressed to perfection, and a beaming, toothy smile. He insisted that Christians who were faithful should be rich, and he said not a word about any kind of sacrifice. It was like watching a Zig Ziglar infomercial with occasional Christian sprinkles on top. In America that's how we like our religion, easy on the theology and guilt trips, heavy on the material blessing and easy paths to obtaining what our possessive hearts desire.

The reason this scene on the TV struck me so strongly is that I had just been reading one of the early church fathers, John Chrysostom. Chrysostom, like Francis of Assisi, was a full-fledged ascetic. His motto was along the lines of "when in doubt, leave it out." What struck me is that Chrysostom and the televangelist were saying diametrically opposite things about what God really wants for us, and what the true gospel entails. Chrysostom is very emphatic—it is only the pagans who strive for material success, prosperity, and the lifestyle of the rich and famous. It is only the pagans who overeat, overbuy, and in general are into supersizing everything from waistlines, to clothing, to houses, to jewelry, to vehicles. Only pagans would be that self-indulgent, in Chrysostom's view. So what we now call the prosperity gospel is, according to Chrysostom, the world's gospel, not the Savior's gospel.

Who is right? Does the Bible preach "God helps those who help themselves" and prosperity for all those who believe hard enough, or does it preach a very different gospel, something like "blessed are you poor, for yours is the kingdom of God" (Luke 6:20)? What does the Bible really say about things like money, private property, prosperity, and wealth? What does the Bible really say about the good life and how to live it? Let me be clear from the outset. I think that *both* the televangelists and Chrysostom have it wrong in some ways, but that clearly Chrysostom is closer to the truth and the real heart of the matter than the prosperity preachers are. I'll explain why as we go along in this little book.

Here I need to hop down from my high horse for a minute and recognize something important that the prosperity preachers are indeed tapping into. People, perhaps especially Christian people, are looking for answers, including spiritual answers about real life issues involving money. They would like to know what God and the Bible have to say about such matters, and to their credit they are looking to the church, or at least to some of its more photogenic ministers, for answers to these questions. Props to the prosperity preachers for trying to help these people in their quest for understanding the material world and material things from a more godly perspective. And we need to be clear that the biblical material is not monolithic on this subject. It is complex. It is thus understandable how some of the biblical material, cited out of context and without nuance, can lead to the errors of the prosperity gospel. We should not assume that all those who listen to its message are just a bunch of greedy people looking for biblical justification for having a lifestyle of conspicuous consumption. This is certainly not universally the case.

Let me add a personal note as well. Most American Christians, myself included, are already wealthy by global and historical standards. To some it will ring hollow for someone like me—who is neither poor nor wealthy by American standards, but is certainly well-off by global standards—to be so severely critical of those who are drawn to the prosperity gospel. One might ask, What's so wrong with the Star Trek motto of "live long and prosper"? Isn't this the hope of most normal people?

These are perfectly fair questions, and they deserve honest answers. The most basic of those honest answers is this: I am striving to do my best not merely to become and be a more biblical, more generous and giving person, but also to de-enculturate myself from the dominant materialistic paradigm that drives our culture. I know perfectly well that this is an ongoing struggle, a definite swimming upstream against the American tidal wave of material possessions. My basic problem with prosperity preachers is that they want to baptize the materialistic orientation of our culture and call it godly and good, call it a blessing from God, when it is often better seen as a temptation of the devil. By placing the emphasis where they do, prosperity gospel preachers neglect the cut-and-thrust of New Testament warnings against such matters, warnings that are spoken over and over again. And let me add that pursuing answers to these sorts of questions is not like playing a game of trivial pursuit. It's actually a matter of spiritual life and death.

Indeed, how one relates to the material world and wealth and health issues reveals where one's ultimate loyalties and priorities lie. It's a matter of the heart, and right now too much of the American church, and perhaps especially the conservative and evangelical church, is suffering from heart disease, from clogged spiritual arteries, indeed from one or another form of idolatry, the lusting after false gods. And of course part of the problem is that the Bible gets sound-bited to support what we already desire to be true.

As a relatively wealthy Christian and a biblical scholar, my most urgent concern is with the flagrant disregard for what the Bible actually says about money and other related subjects. Perhaps we need to go back to square one and build up a whole new biblical view of things like money, wealth, property, tithing, saving, health, pursuing the good life. Perhaps we have totally forgotten—or terribly distorted—what the Bible does say about such things. So our first priority must be to remind ourselves of exactly what the Bible does say or suggest on such subjects, before we try and use the Bible to support our all too convenient preexisting agendas.

Hanging the Picture Straight: A Preview of Coming Attractions

We live in an atomistic age, the age of the sound bite, the quick glimpse, the short summary. The constant cry as we sail a sea of information in the information age is "boil it down," which usually means, at least implicitly, dumb it down or simplify it. It is not surprising, then, that when it comes to a subject as complex as money and wealth distorted approaches to the data are all too common. The temptation is to cherry-pick this or that verse, this or that passage, to justify a preconceived theology of possessions and wealth.

There are ways to avoid such selective misuse of the biblical texts. One, of course, is to look at as much of the text as one can, and resist the temptation to ignore the bits that seem inconvenient for one's favorite theory. In an important study, Sondra Wheeler points out how paying attention to the whole Bible—and not just a favored passage or two—can change the discussion about money. "For example," writes Wheeler, "to an interpreter who finds Luke 12:33 ('sell your possessions and give to the poor') a moral rule requiring complete divestiture, binding on all believers in every time and place, the equally clear injunction 'Do not neglect hospitality' (Heb. 13:2) presents a problem. How can Christians invite strangers into their homes if they are not to own anything?"[1]

Such a canonical or whole-Bible approach requires that we understand the social as well as the literary context of the given injunctions. For example, when we look at Luke 12:33 ("sell your possessions and give to the poor") in the larger context of just Luke's Gospel alone, it is clear that neither Jesus nor Luke intended such an injunction to be universally applied to all persons in all circumstances. But there is no way to know this without careful examination of the larger context, which is precisely what is often missing in today's church discussions about what the Bible says about money. What is interesting about a comprehensive look at the Old Testament and early Jewish literature on the matter of wealth and possessions is that in fact the Jewish literature is not simply all in favor of wealth and abundance. And the New Testament is not simply all against having possessions and some prosperity in life. The evidence is more mixed and complex.

For example, Wheeler summarizes what the Old Testament says about wealth and abundance under four headings:

1. *Wealth as an occasion for idolatry* (Deut. 32:10–18; Isa. 2:6–8; 3:16–24; Jer. 5:7; Ezek. 7:19–20; 16:15–22; Hos. 2:5–9; Amos 6:4–7). The prophets warn about the dangers of wealth leading to idolatry, which is to say unfaithfulness to God, especially to God's call for one's absolute allegiance and trust, relying on God alone as one's source of security.

2. *Wealth as the fruit of injustice* (Isa. 3:14–15; 10:1–3; Mic. 6:10–12; Jer. 5:27–28; Amos 2:6; 4:1–2). The prophetic critique against those who accrue wealth dishonestly and exploitatively is severe. As Wheeler stresses, "not only violence and oppression are condemned [in these texts]: the provisions of the covenant requiring forgiveness of debts, the return of the alienated land to the impoverished in the jubilee year, and the freeing of those sold into slavery are also binding, and to violate them is to invite God's wrath" (cf. Zech. 7:14).[2] This is not to say that wealth and prosperity are always associated with injustice and idolatry.

3. *Wealth as a sign of faithfulness* (Lev. 26:3–10; Deut. 11:13–15; Isa. 54:11–12; 60:9–16; Jer. 33:6–9). "The same Deuteronomistic and prophetic traditions that excoriate the apostasy, oppression, and heartlessness of the rich, promise all manner of abundance as the consequence of fidelity to God and God's covenant."[3] The question then becomes: How can we tell when prosperity is a sign of divine blessing, and when it is a sign of human oppression and injustice? Again, the problem in modern prosperity preaching is that only one side of the biblical witness is presented, and even that is very selectively presented, leading to distortion and wrong emphases.

4. *Wealth as the reward for hard labor* (Prov. 10–21). In the Wisdom literature, labor and its rewards are often contrasted with laziness.[4] It

is very interesting that this fourth Old Testamental theme disappears almost entirely in the New Testament.

What, then, are the basic themes on wealth in the New Testament? Wheeler again lists four:

1. *Wealth as a stumbling block* (Luke 18:18–30). The human impossibility of the rich entering God's kingdom is stressed in all three of the Synoptic Gospels (Matthew, Mark, and Luke). "In the Gospels," Wheeler summarizes, "the concern for material wealth repeatedly thwarts the response to Jesus' preaching, and thus it takes on centrality as the occasion for that failure."[5]

2. *Wealth as a competing object of devotion.* In the Gospels, when a person becomes too attached to possessions, a choice is forced, since one cannot serve both God and mammon (Matt. 6:24; Luke 16:13). The disciples are urged not to collect or store up treasures on earth (Matt. 6:19–21; Luke 12:31), because one's heart follows one's first love. Greed is regularly inveighed against as well, as a form of idolatry (Luke 12:15; cf. Eph. 4:28; Col. 3:6). At the same time, Wheeler aptly points out that it is not as if the New Testament urges the pursuit of poverty as a good in itself: "There is no absolute condemnation of having possessions. If the first and second themes of the New Testament on wealth are that possessions tend to hinder discipleship and that all riches tempt one to trust in them rather than in God, then there is a corollary to both of these. Poverty is not to be sought for itself, or as a guarantor of moral purity, but only as a means of securing the liberty for undivided obedience and loyalty to God's reign. Within the view of reality advocated in the New Testament, literally nothing else matters."[6]

3. *Wealth as a resource for human needs.* This is a very persistent theme in the New Testament. Whether one looks to Paul (Rom. 15:25–27; Gal. 6:6), James (James 2:15–16), or Luke (Acts 2 and 4), all urge liberality. Paul even says that giving money or possessions is a form of obedience to the confession of the gospel (2 Cor. 9:13). Lest we think this only means giving to our fellow Christians, he says that we are to do good to all, but *especially* to the household of faith; Jesus simply instructs us to give to everyone who asks (Matt. 5:42; Luke 6:30). Even an enemy should be fed (Rom. 12:20). These sorts of texts provide a good, positive counterpart that shows that Jesus and various early Christian writers thought it was possible for someone to have possessions and still be a follower of Jesus.

4. *Wealth as a symptom of economic injustice.* This theme carries over from the Old Testament prophetic witness into the New. It is prevalent especially in Luke's Gospel (1:51–53; 4:18–19; 6:21; 16:19–26). The same sort of warning about wealth is also found in the book of Revelation (17:3–4; 18:9–19), where it is contrasted, as in the parable in Luke 18, with the poor pious persons who make it to heaven (Rev. 2:8–10; 7:16–17). One of the corollaries to these warnings is the admonition to avoid treatment that favors the rich more than the poor (James 2:5; 4:1–2; 5:1–6).

The point of this preliminary survey is to show the diverse kinds of material we have, including attitudes, about wealth and possessions in the Bible. Sondra Wheeler's discussion is a good reminder of that diversity. Much depends on context and the difference between the ancient and modern ones, not the least of which is the collectivist nature of all biblical cultures and the radically individualistic and atomistic character of modern Western culture.

We have seen glimpses of what to expect, including a predominant tone of warning in the New Testament when it comes to wealth and possessions. But to understand why we have this sort of varied material, we must look at things in considerably more detail. As we move forward, we will dialogue with Wheeler and several other scholars who have discussed this matter in helpful ways. These scholars are as different in their theologies as the liberation theologian Justo González is to the evangelical Craig Blomberg. What we will discover is that the self-justifying tendency of modern Christians to hoard wealth and live large have absolutely no basis whatsoever in the New Testament. This is especially true in light of the higher and more stringent ethical demands in the New Testament, compared to what we find on such matters in the Old. It is the prophetic witness about the perils of wealth and the dangers of greed and idolatry that are most frequently carried forward from the Hebrew Scriptures into the New Testament witness about money and wealth.

The Plan of This Book

Complex as the biblical material may be, the plan of this book is simple. We will examine in summary form some of the relevant material from the Old Testament, but concentrate on a few New Testament witnesses who say more directly what followers of Jesus ought to think and do about such matters. One of the major problems with using the Old Testament to justify a prosperity gospel for Christians is that Christians aren't under the Mosaic covenant at all anymore! They are called to a higher standard under the new covenant. So in one sense, what the book of Proverbs says to ancient Jews should never be the primary basis for building a Christian understanding of wealth and the like. It has some relevance as background, especially when it is quoted and reaffirmed by New Testament authors. But in general the main source of what Christians ought to think about these things is not the prayer of Jabez in 1 Chronicles 4:10 but the prayer of Jesus—and what a world of difference there is between the Jabez prayer and the Lord's Prayer.

So let's get started. I promise this discussion will not be boring. Indeed, my goal is to make it *rich*, in many surprising ways.

1

"In the Beginning God Created . . ."

Getting Our Bearings

If we have become a people incapable
Of thought, then the brute-thought
Of mere power and mere greed
Will think for us.

If we have become incapable
Of denying ourselves anything,
Then all that we have
Will be taken from us.

If we have no compassion
We will suffer alone, we will suffer
Alone the destruction of ourselves.

—Wendell Berry[1]

Money is a touchy subject. Some people don't want to talk about it at all and others obsess about it—whether they have it or not. So where should we begin to discuss such delicate but essential issues as money and material resources, from a biblical point of view? My suggestion is that we go all the way back to the very beginning to get some perspective and see things from God's point of view. Hence, we are going to go *ad fontes*, back to Genesis 1, to get our bearings and a real running start into the biblical witness on money.

What in Creation?

It is important from the start to recognize that money is just one sort of asset, one sort of material good that exists in this world, and from a theological point of view all such "stuff" should be discussed together. The rationale for such a discussion comes from the very first chapter of the Bible, where we read the following: "In the beginning, God created the heavens and the earth" and then it goes on to say at the end of the chapter "and God saw all that he had made, and it was good" (Gen. 1:1 and 31). All things—the whole material universe and everything in it—are created by God. Equally important, all things were created good. Trees are good, the sun is good, animals are good, food is good, minerals are good, people are good, and so on. There is nothing inherently evil about any material thing, not even money. Of course it is true that human beings have the capacity to take a good thing and turn it into something harmful and even wicked, like turning the coca plant into cocaine.

But there is an important corollary that comes with the notion that God created all things, and made them all good. That corollary is that *all things ultimately belong to God.* They do not "belong" in the fullest sense to human beings. As the psalmist puts it, "The earth is the Lord's and the fullness thereof, the world and all who dwell there" (Ps. 24:1). Properly speaking, God is the only owner of all things, whether born or made, whether natural or humanly fashioned. This sounds simple and obvious enough, but all too often we fail to think about money and material possessions in this proper theological way. And that failure leads to a host of problems. Apparently it is easy to forget that we brought nothing with us into this world, and even if we are buried with our pink Cadillacs we can't actually take them with us. Perhaps you've heard the humorous story about a man who was about to die so he liquidated all his assets, turning them into gold bricks. He required his family to pack the bricks in two suitcases and bury them with him. When he arrived at the pearly gates St. Peter met him and immediately noted the oddity that this man had come to heaven with luggage. "What's in the suitcases?" inquired Peter. The man proudly opened his suitcases. Peter stared into them nonplussed, then said: "You brought pavement up here? Pavement?"

Christians can have some pretty odd notions about the issue of ownership in this world. What a proper understanding of the Genesis creation story reminds us of is that God is the maker and owner of all things, and so, as the story of Adam and Eve makes evident, we are but stewards of God's property. Our task is to be good stewards of property we do not own. Adam and Eve were to fill the earth and subdue it, they were to be fruitful and multiply, they were to tend and take care of the garden, but they were not to think they owned the world just because they worked in the world. And this brings us to another important point.

In modern Western culture we place a high value on work, which is fine, but one of the philosophical assumptions that can come with such values is that we assume that we own what we earn or buy. From a biblical point of view this is extremely problematic. There isn't any necessary correlation between hard work and ownership. Think, for example, of all the hard work that went into building the pyramids in Egypt. Most of the workers were slaves, and they had no delusions that because they built the pyramids they owned the pyramids. No, they believed that both the pyramids and they themselves belonged to Pharaoh! In this sense (excepting of course that Pharaoh is not God), they had a more biblical worldview of work than most of us do. Our hard work may be well rewarded or not. It may produce prosperity or not. But until we see all that we receive, whether by earning it or receiving it without work, as a gift from God, a gift we should use knowing who the true owner of the gift is, we will not be thinking biblically about such matters.

The Misguided Notion of Human Ownership and Private Property

A theology of human ownership creates all sorts of problems: rival claims for a plot of land, tussles over wills and inheritances, efforts to buy up as much property as possible, remembering the mantra "location, location, location." It leads to assumptions that we are what we own, or what we supposedly own. We create bumper stickers with slogans like "Whoever dies with the most toys wins." But alas, there is no cheating death on the basis of the accumulation of things.

Of course, some ancient cultures literally believed that we can take it with us when we die. For example, the excavation of the great King

Tut's tomb in the Egyptian Valley of the Kings revealed a wealth of treasure, clothes, chariots, and food. But the mummy of the Pharaoh is still in the museum of Egyptology in Cairo, and all his bling is now on display there and elsewhere. So not only could he not take it with him, he will not find it in the tomb should he finally rise from the dead and go back there to visit!

The biblical theology of creation is a negation of theories of "private" property and "public" property, our theories of individual ownership and collective or governmental ownership. The biblical view is that only God is the owner of the universe, because God created and fashioned it in the first place, and then *loaned* it to us to use properly. One of the practical implications of this theological outlook is that one must always ask questions about any use of material things, such as: Is this what God intended for us to do with this material? Will this use reflect good stewardship of God's resources? Will this or that use of property or money glorify God and edify people?

Why should we ask such questions? Because of the story in Genesis 3, which reminds us that we are all fallen creatures. We have all fallen short of the glory of God. We all have an infinite capacity for rationalizing decisions about money and possessions. We all have infinite capacity for self-justification. Since the fall we have all experienced "the heart turned in upon itself."

One of the saddest and least biblical corollaries of the theory of private property is the notion of charity. I once preached a sermon with the title "Charity is a Sin." It certainly got the audience's attention. The basic assumption behind the concept of charity is "what's mine is mine, and if I share it with you, I am being charitable or generous"— as if sharing the wealth is optional. But alas for such ideas, the Bible is replete with *commandments*, not mere suggestions, about giving to others, taking care of the poor, sacrificing for others, and so on. But if giving is required of God's people, and if God is the owner of all property, then what should we make of the whole business of tithing? Doesn't tithing mean that the 90 percent I don't give to God belongs to me, by rights? I'm glad you asked.

Blest Be the Tithe That Binds

"A tithe of everything from the land, whether grain from the soil or fruit from the trees belongs to the Lord; it is holy to the Lord," reads

Leviticus 27:30. It may come as something of a surprise but there are more remarks in the Old Testament about tithing than there are about the afterlife. But we can't very well understand what tithing is really all about without the proper theological context. It is in light of a particular theology of creation that we must evaluate what is said about tithing in the Old Testament. God doesn't *need* material things, but God requires a tithe of the firstfruits, the first good portion of a crop, before people can use any of the rest. Indeed, in texts like Exodus 13 God requires a consecration of the first born son. God doesn't just want our resources, God wants us!

Why is it that a tithe of *everything* is required by God, even spices and condiments like dill, mint, and cumin (see Matt. 23:23)? The answer is simple—because it is a reminder to God's people that everything belongs to God. Everything! It's not a matter of parceling things out between God's portion and our portion, God's property and our property. *It all belongs to God*, and the tithing of the very firstfruits of any and all crops and other things is a constant reminder of this fact.

What is amazing about the teachings on tithing in the Old Testament is not that God demands a tithe but that God does not demand it *all* back, since it all belongs to God. Behold the graciousness and generosity of God, who wants his people to be able to have life, and live it to the full. Not, however, at the expense of forgetting to whom it all belongs.

But should Christians tithe? This is a much debated subject, and in my view the answer is no. If we carefully read the books of Leviticus and Deuteronomy we discover that tithing requirements are juxtaposed with requirements as varied as stoning disobedient children, leaving the edge of your grain field for gleaning by the poor, avoiding tattoos (yes, that's in there too), and a host of other commandments that Christians haven't thought about keeping for a long time. Intuitively, even Christians who are not very biblically literate know that we are not under the Mosaic covenant anymore. We don't live our lives on the basis of the Mosaic law given to the Hebrews so many centuries ago. We are under the new covenant inaugurated by Jesus, and it has many commandments, *but tithing is not one of them*. The basic rule of guidance about such things is that if the Old Testament commandment is reaffirmed in the New Testament for Christians, then we are still obligated to do it. If it is not, then we are not.

Someone may object and say: "But wait, Jesus spoke about tithing dill, mint, and cumin in Matthew 23:23. That's in the New Testament." It is, but to whom are Jesus's remarks made? Notice the context: "Woe to you teachers of the law and Pharisees, you hypocrites. You give a tenth of your spices, mint, dill, and cumin. But you have neglected the more important matters of the law—justice, mercy, and faithfulness. You should have practiced the latter, without neglecting the former." Here Jesus is instructing the Pharisees, not his own disciples, much less Christians after Easter. Jesus wants the Pharisees to be consistent if they are going to keep the Mosaic covenant, which they have promised to do. Clearly the Mosaic covenant commands tithing. But it is striking that nowhere does Jesus tell his own disciples to tithe. In fact, what he tells them is something more radical than giving a tenth of their income, as we will see in a subsequent chapter.

The most we can glean from this passage by way of application to any Christian is that if a person is genuinely a Jewish Christian and believes that in order to be a good witness to one's fellow Jews one must keep Torah, then indeed that person has thereby committed himself or herself to tithing. But let me be clear: Paul says that even Jewish Christians like himself are no longer required to keep Torah, though as a missionary practice they may do so (see 1 Cor. 9).

To me, one of the great ironies about preachers who insist that their congregants should all tithe is that at the very same time they ignore what else is said about money or resources and their use in these same biblical contexts. I am referring to what is said about usury in the Pentateuch (the first five books of the Old Testament). The term *usury* comes from the Latin *usuria*, and in its original sense it refers to any charging of interest. Ancient cultures held a variety of opinions on this matter, and interestingly the Hebrew Scriptures had the most strict or stringent view. Wikipedia summarizes the topic of usury as follows:

> "Most early religious systems in the ancient Near East, and the secular codes arising from them, did not forbid usury. These societies regarded inanimate matter as alive, like plants, animals and people, and capable of reproducing itself. Hence if you lent 'food money,' or monetary tokens of any kind, it was legitimate to charge interest. Food money in the shape of olives, dates, seeds or animals was lent out as early as c. 5000 BC, if not earlier. . . . Among the Mesopotamians, Hittites, Phoenicians and Egyptians, interest was legal and often fixed by the state. But the Jews took a different view of the matter."[2]
>
> The Torah and later sections of the Hebrew Bible criticize interest-taking, but interpretations of the Biblical prohibition vary. One com-

mon understanding is that Israelites are forbidden to charge interest upon loans made to other Israelites, but allowed to charge interest on transactions with non-Israelites. However, the Hebrew Bible itself gives numerous examples where this provision was evaded. Usury (in the original sense of any interest) was denounced by a number of spiritual leaders and philosophers of ancient times, including Plato, Aristotle, Cato, Cicero, Seneca, Plutarch, Aquinas, Muhammad, Moses, Philo and Gautama Buddha.[3]

The texts in question are Exodus 22:25, Leviticus 25:35–37, and Deuteronomy 23:20–21, and they all seem quite clear that lending at interest is something that God's people should not do. Deuteronomy 23 makes an exception if one is lending to a foreigner, and it is fair to say the first two texts are especially concerned with not bilking the poor. Nonetheless, the principle is established that believers should not lend money at interest to other believers. Of course such rules were evaded at times by God's people, but notice Ezekiel's complaint at a much later time that usury, and especially excessive interest, is unjust (Ezek. 18:8–17). It should be borne in mind as well that when we find in the New Testament the idea of "give with no thought of return," this extends the principle of no usury even further. In general, the New Testament takes an even more demanding approach to what should be done with our resources than the Old Testament.

My point in bringing all this to light is that I do not hear preachers urging the practice of not charging interest while they are busy stressing tithing. The inconsistency here is glaring. But in fact Christians are not bound to any of these Old Testament provisions, including tithing, since we are no longer under the Mosaic covenant.

Following the Money?

At this point in the discussion some will remark that the Old Testament says a good deal about being prosperous and even occasionally speaks about wealth, but not about money per se. That is the case because ancient economies were not money-based economies, and they were certainly not free market capitalist economies. As we shall see in later chapters, money was beginning to play a larger economic role in Jesus's era, but even then it operated mainly within the context of a barter or "bargain and exchange" economy. Money was used for paying taxes and tolls, but less frequently for everyday business.

There is another huge factor often overlooked in discussions of what the Bible says about money and wealth. All ancient economies, especially those of major empires and powers, were dependent on slave labor. One estimate even suggests that by the time Paul and Peter visited Rome in the 60s AD, 50 percent of all the workers in the city were slaves.[4] Today we may jest that working for minimum wage is "slave labor," but slave labor was literally predominant in the ancient biblical world. We will discuss these matters at greater length in subsequent chapters, but here the point is that there are vast differences between our own world and the economic world in which the Bible was written. If we are to properly understand the key New Testament texts about money, we need to keep in mind the fundamental factors that economically distinguished those cultures from ours.

Wealth in the Old Testament

Despite the continued efforts of some prosperity preachers to say otherwise, the Old Testament actually does not provide real justification for the conspicuous accumulation, much less conspicuous consumption, of material things. Indeed, there are frequent warnings about the dangers of wealth, and wealth is sometimes associated with idolatry.[5] For example, in Ezekiel 7:19–20 wealth is said to be the stumbling block that led the Israelites into iniquity and idolatry. Also strongly criticized is the making of idols out of precious metals, which presupposes possession of considerable wealth. Deuteronomy 32:15 warns about God's people growing fat and unfaithful as a result of their prosperity.

Not surprisingly, the prophets are especially incensed with the wealthy when they deprive and cheat others, including the poor. Micah 6:10–12 accuses the wealthy of being full of violence and completely dishonest in their business practices, in this case by using unfair scales, weights, and balances. Isaiah 10:1–3 repeatedly complains about lawmakers who make statutes that "turn aside the needy from justice and rob the poor of their rights." There is in fact an enormous amount of complaint about stealing from widows and orphans in the Old Testament, including in Isaiah 10. Isaiah 3:14–15 accuses the elders, the leaders of the people, of grinding the poor into the dust of the ground, using their labor but depriving them of necessary food and drink, and even stealing what little the poor have in their homes.

It is in this context that we should begin to evaluate the promises of rain and good crops that come in texts like Leviticus 26:3–5 and Deuteronomy 11:13–15. Notice that in these texts the promises are conditional upon keeping God's "every statute," or keeping the commandments faithfully over one's lifetime. It is imperative that we understand here that these promises are not unconditional, and they are not made on the basis of merely asking God for a blessing, or merely praying for a blessing. Consider for example Deuteronomy 11:13–15: "If you will only heed God's every commandment—loving the Lord your God and serving him with all your heart and soul, then he will give the rain for your land in season . . . and you will gather in your grain . . . and you will eat your fill." Clearly, this is not actually a promise that the pious will get rich. It is a promise of a good crop, and of no one having too little to eat. Sometimes texts like Isaiah 60:8–12 (with "silver and gold" delivered to the Israelites) are brought into the discussion of prosperity. But we need to realize that the promises here are eschatological (or end-time) promises made to a people in exile. They are not promises of prosperity for just anyone in any situation, whenever they might ask God for it. Of exactly the same sort are the promises in Jeremiah 33:6–9, which speaks of an "abundance of prosperity and security."

Sometimes texts like Psalm 37:4 ("delight yourself in the Lord, and he will give you the desires of the heart") are also touted as prosperity guarantees for the pious. The immediate assumption of the prosperity preachers is that the psalms must be referring to material goods and possessions. But again, context is crucial. What the psalm as a whole promises is not worldly wealth. Instead, it says that God will help his people dwell safely in the land, he will make their righteousness (not their jewelry) shine like the sun, and he will make the justice of their cause apparent. This same psalm goes on to add, "Better the little the righteous have than the wealth of the many wicked." Pursuing the contrast further, the psalmist adds "the wicked borrow and do not repay, but the righteous give generously." This brings us back to the key verse, which is verse 4. In context, what is the "desire of the heart of a righteous person"? Surely the answer is the Lord himself, and to be vindicated against the wicked by divine intervention. This is hardly a psalm that supports prosperity theology.

Psalm 25 is another text often cited by preachers of the prosperity gospel. This is a psalm of distress, crying out to God to rescue the psalmist from his tormentors. It is said that those who truly revere and serve the Lord he will instruct in his ways, and "they will spend their days in prosperity and their descendants will inherit the land." Again we have a conditional promise, based on reverence for God. Note as well that this same psalm speaks of the affliction of the person in question, and of the loneliness and troubles. Clearly prosperity is not seen as coming without trials and suffering.

What we can say about such texts is that while prosperity *may* be a mark of God's favor, this is not always so, since it can also be a mark of one's wickedness. We will have occasion to talk at length about some of the proverbs and aphorisms of Solomon and others in the next chapter. They deserve more lengthy treatment since they are so often the cornerstone texts misused to support an unbiblical view of prosperity and wealth.

The Prayer of Jabez Revisited

First Chronicles 4:9–10 could be forgiven for being called the text that roared, once Bruce Wilkinson got his hands on it and wrote a little book called *The Prayer of Jabez*. This book, which was released in 2000, sold nine million copies in its first two years in print (over seventeen million now), becoming one of the best selling Christian books of all time. But what exactly does 1 Chronicles 4:9–10 say that caused such a sensation? In the midst of apparently innocuous genealogies we find these two verses: "Jabez was more honorable than his brothers. His mother had named him Jabez saying: 'I gave birth to him in pain.' Jabez cried out to the God of Israel, 'Oh that you would bless me and enlarge my territory! Let your hand be with me, and keep me from harm so that I will be free from pain.' And God granted his request." That's all there is to the story and the context. It is preceded and followed by unrelated genealogy.

What should we make of this brief narrative? First of all, we should notice that the theme of the narrative is pain. It's about pain in childbirth and a prayer to be free from pain (which may imply that Jabez was in pain at the time of the prayer). Further, the name Jabez sounds like the Hebrew word for pain. Perhaps here a more literal rendering with some Hebrew transliteration will help.

Jabez was more honorable than his brothers; and his mother called his name Jabez [y'bts], saying, "Because I bore him in pain [b'tsb]." Jabez called on the God of Israel, saying, "Oh that you would bless me and enlarge my border, and that your hand might be with me, and that you would keep me from harm so that it might not hurt me ['tsby]!" And God granted what he asked. (1 Chron. 4:9–10)

In ancient times wordplays were a common practice when it came to bestowing a name. Notice that our man is called Jabez rather than Jazeb, which would be more nearly the Hebrew word for pain. This seems to be the prayer of a rather poor or indigent person, who barely has enough land for survival and is also in danger. But notice: *Nothing suggests that when the prayer was answered God made Jabez a wealthy man, because nothing suggests that Jabez requested wealth at all*. What he may well have requested is simply adequate land and safety to make a living and take care of his family. What these two little verses definitely do suggest is that God answers prayer, particularly prayers of his faithful people who are crying out for basic necessities like safety and the ability to make a living. Nothing here suggests that God intends to make the rich richer, simply because they ask and trust that God is capable of giving such material blessings.

And So? Good Bearings and Red Herrings

In this brief chapter we have taken time to get our bearings for our study of money and wealth in the New Testament. I do not really think that the Old Testament differs significantly from the New Testament about such matters, but it is important to deal in a general way with some red herrings, such as the prayer of Jabez, that do not really provide us with a theology of prosperity in the modern sense. And it was especially crucial to frame our discussion properly, in light of the theology of creation and the notion that, properly speaking, God is the owner of all things.

Along the way we noted how the practice of tithing is grounded in the theology of creation in the Old Testament and is a requirement only for those who are under the Mosaic covenant. I introduced the idea that ancient economies were not like modern ones for a variety of reasons. I stressed that money itself is not much discussed in the Old Testament because ancient economies were not money-based. The way money functioned in barter economies was very different from the way it functions today. It is ironic that so many modern ministers insist that Christians should tithe, but they totally ignore what the same portions of the Old Testament say about usury—lending money with interest—never mind lending it with exorbitant interest.

If, however, there are texts in the Old Testament thought to provide a basis for a prosperity theology and the accumulation of wealth, they are the proverbs and aphorisms found in the book of Proverbs. We turn to this Wisdom literature next, and to its cousin in a very different mood, the book of Ecclesiastes.

2

A King's Ransom

Proverbial Wisdom on Wealth

The wealth of the rich is their fortified city, but poverty is the ruin of the poor.

—Proverbs 10:14

Wealth is worthless in the day of wrath, but righteousness delivers from death.

—Proverbs 11:4

Money is better than poverty, if only for financial reasons.

—Woody Allen

Perhaps no section of the Old Testament has been more misused in the contemporary discussion of prosperity and wealth than the book of Proverbs. After all, doesn't it say in Proverbs 10:22 that "the blessing of the Lord brings wealth, and he adds no trouble to it"? Of course in this same collection of proverbs and aphorisms we read, "Those who trust in their riches will fall, but the righteous will thrive like a green leaf" (Prov. 11:28). Proverbs, and its dark twin Ecclesiastes (often ignored in the whole discussion of prosperity and wealth today), will bear close scrutiny as we work our way towards the teaching of Jesus

29

and his followers on wealth and money. That is especially the case since Jesus and his followers were deeply indebted to the Wisdom literature of the Hebrew Scriptures and early Judaism.

The Wisdom of Solomon

Understanding Wisdom literature requires patience. This is so in part because much of Wisdom literature involves indirect speech— metaphors, similes, figures of speech, images, personifications, riddles and the like. It's a kind of literature that seeks to persuade not by demanding assent but by making assertions that cause the audience to rethink its worldview.[1] Sometimes wisdom comes from "above," both in the sense of revelatory wisdom from God and in the sense of it coming from the higher echelons of society—say, for example, from a king such as Solomon.

This is the sort of wisdom we find to some degree in the book of Proverbs, and what one must always bear in mind in reading proverbs is that the assumed social context is a society that is functioning relatively well, that is, in a basically God-honoring way. In such a biblical society it could be said that "the Lord does not allow the righteous to go hungry, but he thwarts the craving of the wicked" (Prov. 10:3). How very different this is from the society observed by Qoheleth, the narrator of Ecclesiastes, who at a later time in Hebrew history bemoans, "If you see the poor oppressed in a district, and justice and rights denied, do not be surprised at such things. . . . Those who love money never have enough; those who love wealth are never satisfied with their income. This too is meaningless" (Eccles. 5:8–10).

In other words, *proverbs and aphorisms are always situation specific.* They are not some sort of universal lucky charms that work in all circumstances, regardless of the social context in which one lives. They describe what happens under particular, limited conditions and only when a person is in right (or wrong) relationship with the God of the universe. The possession of wealth is just as often seen as a sign of wickedness as it is of righteousness, of connivance as of blessing, if we bother to read through all Wisdom literature and not simply sound-bite our favorite proverbs. In short, a person cannot tell one's standing with God from the size of one's bank account, though certainly it is true that sometimes material things are said to be a blessing from God.

Perhaps it will help to define the term *wisdom* here at the outset. *Hokmah* in the Hebrew, or *sophia* in the Greek, can refer to a variety of things. In the Old Testament it refers to at least five different kinds of wisdom. One kind is *political wisdom*, or knowing the politic thing to do in a specific difficult situation (1 Kings 5:21). Another is an *encyclopedic knowledge of nature* (1 Kings 4:33), with the assumption that knowledge provides clues about human nature and the world of proper human relationships. In other instances wisdom is *the gift of discernment or critical judgment*, knowing the right thing to do in a difficult situation (1 Kings 3:16–28). It can also indicate *a saying or riddle or proverb that reveals a deeper truth or secret about life*, providing insight into what truly matters or how things truly work. Finally, wisdom can refer simply to *skill, expertise, or artisanship* (1 Chron. 22:15; 2 Chron. 5:7).

Usually in Proverbs, and in the Old Testament in general, the third definition listed above—wisdom as discernment—comes to the fore. The greater portion of the book of Proverbs is about knowing how to read the moral character and ways of one's society, and then live according to those moral structures so that one does not merely survive but actually thrives.

The proverbs were coined by sages, and often a shrewd king himself would be the creator of such compact doses of wisdom. It appears that most ancient courts employed sages who served as counselors and scribes of the king. Second Samuel 16:23 and 1 Kings 4:1–19 and 10:1 suggest that Israelite kings had such counselors or sages on their staffs. But for the most part these counselors were expected to offer wisdom of the first sort listed above—political wisdom—rather than general guidance for life. We should not, however, look only to the royal court for the source of this wisdom material, for some of it clearly comes from the home (for example, advice of a father to a son) or the collected wisdom of village elders and the like. The fact that we have some of the wise sayings of the Egyptian sage Amenemope in our book of Proverbs (Prov. 22:17–23:11, except 19:23, 26–27) reminds us that wisdom was considered to be universal, so that one could learn from other parallel cultures about the art of living prudently. It appears that court sages/scribes collected wisdom from the entire region, and some of these collected materials are now found in our book of Proverbs (see, for example, Prov. 30–31, on the sayings of Agur or King Lemuel).

Above all, we need to keep in mind that in ancient biblical cultures literacy was chiefly the property of the elite, a luxury available primarily to royalty and their counselors and sages. The persons who had the time, energy, and money to search out wisdom and write things down were either the socially elite or those who were in close association with them. The association could be as simple as being part of a wealthy estate, but it could also be as grand as being a member of a royal court.

We also need to keep in mind that ancient Hebrew culture was an oral culture, and so the wisdom that originated in the home might well be conveyed orally into other social settings, eventually ending up in the hands of court scribes. In addition, it is helpful to make a distinction between the sages who coined proverbs and the scribes who wrote them down, though surely there were some sages who were also scribes. Ecclesiastes 12:9–11 provides clues as to how we got this literature in the first place. It was oral tradition, which was collected by sages like Qoheleth, written down, and arranged or grouped in various ways.

The ethos that the book of Proverbs exudes is a time, place, and social setting of relative prosperity. Thus it is probably right to conclude that a socially elite setting is the context out of which this collection of wise sayings was generated, and more importantly, that it often reflects an elite point of view—even that of a king. As Robert Gordis concludes,

> Wisdom literature . . . was fundamentally the product of the upper classes in society, who lived principally in the capital, Jerusalem. . . . As is to be expected, the upper classes were conservative in their outlook, basically satisfied with the status quo and opposed to change. Their conservatism extended to every sphere of life, and permeated their religious ideas, as well as their social, economic and political attitudes. What is most striking is that this basic conservatism is to be found among the unconventional Wisdom teachers as well [e.g., Qoheleth]."[2]

Proverbs as a whole reflect the distillation of wisdom over time, often over many generations, and not just the isolated insights of one particular individual. This is why most proverbs are anonymous.

An aphorism is different. Aphorisms provide the unique insight of a creative individual like a Solomon or an Agur or an Amenemope. Proverbs and aphorisms are both compact wisdom material. James

Crenshaw calls them short sentences based on long experience containing a truth.[3] Often both proverbs and aphorisms involve the use of oral and aural devices such as rhythm, rhyme, alliteration, or assonance. All of these devices make them more memorable.

Generally speaking, an aphorist offers individual insight that may go against the flow of received traditional wisdom, but a coiner of proverbs speaks from and for the status quo of long received tradition. We will call the former sort of material counter-order wisdom and the latter traditional wisdom. What we have in the book of Proverbs is traditional wisdom, coined by members of the social elite. This is how things look from the top during a time of general prosperity and peace. What we have in the book of Ecclesiastes, however, is counter-order wisdom, a dissenting opinion from outside the elite circle. Counter-order wisdom is generally offered at a time of considerable social trauma and dislocation.

The importance of this observation for our study of the New Testament wisdom material is that Jesus and his followers mostly spoke counter-order wisdom, wisdom where the last becomes first and traditional values are often turned on their head. This is a wisdom that reflects the in-breaking of the kingdom of God, the divine, saving activity of God. It follows from this that if we simply try to apply preexilic wisdom meant for Israelite society to modern Christian life, without taking into account the difference in social setting and orientation, we will likely misuse these proverbs and aphorisms. Furthermore, this last typical Christian hermeneutical maneuver reflects a rejection of the counter-order wisdom of Jesus and his followers regarding the dangers of money and wealth. We will say more about this when we discuss Jesus's own views on these subjects.

Wisdom in the biblical tradition reflects a belief in one God who revealed himself both through nature and through the special revelation of the Bible. According to the Hebrew sages there were three ways a person could acquire wisdom: through the careful scrutiny of nature and human nature; through learning from one's elders the accumulated deposit of wisdom of previous generations; and through encounter with God, who gives special revelation in such an encounter (Prov. 8; Job 40–41). In the Hebrew tradition this required the development of reason and the intellect, but wisdom was believed to start with God and one's relationship with God: "Reverence for the Lord is the beginning of wisdom" (Prov. 1:7). Consequently, it is an error to talk about the secular character of wisdom in the book of Proverbs. Theocentric or God-centered thinking undergirds all of what is said in Proverbs.

Here I add as well that proverbial wisdom was only one sort of biblical wisdom. As such it had its limitations and weaknesses, as was acknowledged in later Wisdom literature such as Ecclesiastes and Job. In a time of social dislocation, proverbial wisdom was vulnerable to skepticism, to the insight that these proverbs and aphorisms were *not always true, that one size did not fit all social situations.* It was also vulnerable to the insights gained from noting that sometimes even the righteous suffered and experienced poverty, and this was not a negative comment or reflection on their lack of faith. Job is a lengthy meditation on the subject of how the righteous may well suffer.

In other words, when times are out of joint, when there is social dysfunction, war, trauma, famine, and the like, commonsense wisdom simply does not work and proverbs look like dubious platitudes. For example, there is absolutely no point in preaching the prosperity gospel to Christian refugees in camps in Darfur. It will sound like, and indeed will be, a false gospel: their social situation does not allow normal hard work and human ingenuity to bear fruit, as they can in times of peace. During hard times one needs revelatory wisdom, special insight from above, because merely studying received human wisdom is inadequate.

I must also point out that the book of Proverbs (like Ecclesiastes and Job) is based on a particular theology of creation, as we discussed in chapter 1, and what is said about wealth, money, and prosperity reflects this theology. Accordingly, wisdom is believed to be inherent in creation; the study of creation yields godly answers about life. This is why we have sayings that urge a person to go to an anthill and watch the labor of the ants, or consider the stars as God's handiwork, and so on (cf. Prov. 6:6–8; Ps. 8). What is interesting about biblical wisdom is that it draws most of its lessons from the human sphere, not from the realm of inanimate matter, and only secondarily from the realm of subhuman creatures.

There is an order that is good, true, and beautiful encoded in creation, but humans are seldom able to see this larger design. Ironically, what is learned when humans scrutinize the world is how much we do not know, and thus we learn our human limitations (this is the function of Job 38). Such a theology of creation presumes that the faculty of human conscience is real and can be appealed to, and that human beings are capable of rational and moral choices. But of course all the proverbs about fools and their folly show that people can choose poorly as well.

Juxtapositions of diametrical opposites are, among other things, meant to prevent cherry-picking particular wisdom sayings about wealth or riches. For example, Proverbs 26:4–5 first advises not speaking to a fool in his folly, then turns around and advises doing so under certain situations. This pairing raises the important issue of how proverbs are meant to function. Are they seen as timeless truths, valid in any and all situations, or timely truths that are valid in certain sorts of specific situations? It seems clear from the paradoxical sayings that they are intended to have a dialogical (or back-and-forth) rather than a purely didactic function. Proverbs are meant to provide a rule of thumb under certain conditions. Either piece of advice in Proverbs 26:4–5 might be appropriate in a given situation.

It is fair to say that the moral values inculcated in Proverbs are those already urged in the Pentateuch, namely commitment to God and God's divine order, to love justice, honesty, caring for the poor and needy, accepting life as a gift from God, and to despising and avoiding what is wicked and evil. This means that the sages concluded that the wisdom one could discern from nature or human nature (what theologians call general revelation) is in several respects little different from the revelation in Torah that comes directly from God.

One of the major problems with talking about the wealth aphorisms and proverbs in isolation is that they do not exist in isolation. They are offered in the context of discussing, for example, whether or not a person is righteous. Our modern discussions about wealth too rarely note these moral connections. It is not just any suppliant who is said to receive the blessings mentioned in Proverbs, but more specifically the God-fearing, righteous person. In other words, it is not just a matter of praying the prayer of Jabez or simply asking God for material increase. There is so much more involved, like being a righteous person and *not* having an acquisitive heart. Bearing these things in mind, we are now prepared to turn to some of the specific aphorisms of Solomon, and some of the related proverbs.

Solomon's Sagacious Sayings

Let us begin by considering some of the material in Proverbs 10:1–22:6, traditionally associated with Solomon. Proverbs 10:4 says, "Lazy hands make for poverty, but diligent hands bring wealth." This saying does not stand alone. I stress this because just before it we read, "The Lord does not allow the righteous to go hungry" (10:3a). The producer of this aphorism in 10:4 assumes something about the character of the one addressed, something beyond his or her industriousness. The further proof of this conclusion is found on the other side of this saying: "Blessings crown the head of the righteous" (10:6). In this passage virtue is inculcated not by command but by giving examples of behavior and its consequences. I do not mean natural consequences of a cause and effect sort, but rather divine consequences in which *God* blesses certain kinds of persons and behavior. What is presupposed is that there is a moral structure to reality, such that certain kinds of actions normally have particular, predictable consequences, or at least rewards. The moral act-consequence schema is made clear in Proverbs 10:9 and its near twin in 28:18. According to these sayings, one who walks with integrity has more security in life.

If more proof were needed that prosperity is linked to righteousness in the proverbs, we have Proverbs 10:16: "The wages of the righteous bring them life, but the income of the wicked bring them punishment," which immediately follows the aphorism about the wealth of the rich being their fortified city. As we have noted, the sayings about wealth in Proverbs presuppose an audience that has property and a real prospect of prosperity. They do not refer to or address slaves or the indigent. After another reference to the righteous in Proverbs 10:21, we then have the aphorism that "The blessing of the Lord brings wealth" (10:22). What becomes clear as one reads the whole of Proverbs 10 is that piety, righteousness, long life, security, and prosperity are all associated with one another, as are folly, wickedness, ruin, and a short life. And again, all of this is in a context that encourages people of relative wealth, or those who have the possibility of being people of wealth. The audience is not just anyone.

One of the stock characters that appears in Proverbs is the sluggard, or lazy person. This is not the same person as the fool, who is not dim-witted but rather someone who has poor moral judgment. The sluggard appears in Proverbs 10:26, as well as many other places in this book (6:6–8; 10:4; 12:24, 27; 19:15; 21:25). The sluggard is portrayed as useless, restless, and helpless. Life is just too much of an effort for such a person. What we learn from such stock characters is that sages had little patience with either the lazy or the morally obtuse or unwise. The other side of this is the belief that hard work will normally be rewarded, as will good moral judgment.

Proverbs 26:27 is one of the familiar fear/reverence of the Lord sayings, and here it is connected with long life, or at least adding length to life. No doubt the author knew there were exceptions to this rule. Sometimes the good and righteous do die young. The point, however, is that long life is a blessing of God, and God often gives it to one who reveres him. Typically, and in a normal set of circumstances, the righteous can expect their good plans to come to fruition—when the world is operating reasonably closely to the way God intends.

What is perhaps most interesting and surprising is that the sage is addressing the ordinary, day-to-day, even secular life. He is not addressing cultic religion (or the rituals of worship), but how one should conduct one's daily affairs as a godly person. It needs also to be stressed that our author offers no economic scheme, proffers no surefire method of getting rich, and does not promise that God will give large material blessings to whoever asks. And note that even the sages do not think that wealth provides any armor against the day of judgment: only righteousness can do that. Proverbs 11:4 says, "Wealth is worthless in the Day of Wrath, but righteousness delivers from death." Clearly enough, righteousness is seen as something to be inculcated and striven for, whereas wealth is merely a sometime bonus or byproduct of pious living and hard work.

Proverbs 14:4 is interesting in many respects. In the Hebrew, it reads literally, "No oxen, empty manger, strong bull, much money." While there is less work and less mess when one has no ox, nevertheless there is much greater gain when one has a good bull. A healthy bull can sire many calves, and so make considerable profit for the owner. The point of the last half of the saying, then, is that to make wealth or money, sacrifices are necessary—investments of time, energy, and resources must be made. We do not have anything remotely like a get-rich-quick scheme in Proverbs. I must stress again that the juxtaposition of seemingly contradictory proverbs reminds us that the sages knew that there were always exceptions to these generalizations about everyday life. By juxtaposing apparently opposite sayings, the sages are reminding that no one of these sayings universally applies—it depends on the circumstances and the context.

It is, I feel, important to state more explicitly before we move on to the book of Ecclesiastes that we do not have aphorisms for slaves or the poor here. The use of this material in our own time to instill dreams of grandeur that are most often unrealizable for those who are indigent is irresponsible and abusive. Even worse is the use of such material in a name-it-and-claim-it—"if you only have faith enough"[4]—kind of mode, such that when prosperity does not suddenly appear in a person's life one is led to question one's own faith, and indeed the role of faith at all in such matters. That the proverbs and aphorisms we find in Old Testament Wisdom literature are limited in their application to middle and upper-class persons will become even more clear as we turn our focus to the book of Ecclesiastes.

Ecclesiastes: And Now for Something Completely Different

How does one respond to life's emergencies? Think of what happened when the stock market crashed in 1929, and banks closed all over America. Suddenly, people who had been led to believe that their savings were secure in banks learned that even banks were not absolutely safe. In more recent times some Americans have learned this hard lesson during the downturn in the economy and bank closures in 2008. When a crisis comes, wisdom looks different. And what we have in Ecclesiastes is wisdom for rough times, which we call counter-order wisdom.

While Job addresses the crisis situation of a person who suddenly encounters enormous suffering, though he is a righteous and good person, that story is about what happens to a particular individual. In Ecclesiastes, however, it's not that one individual's boat has suddenly and unfairly sunk. Rather, the whole ocean is now in turmoil and everyone's boat is endangered, if not swamped. So it is that Ecclesiastes offers a fundamental challenge to the sort of generalizations one finds in Proverbs. What is especially challenged in this book is the act-consequence schema found in Proverbs.[5]

Ecclesiastes seems to be written at a time when money is coming more to the fore as a significant element in the economic situation. Most scholars have suggested, rightly I think, that this is one of the chronologically later books in the Old Testament canon. There is a skeptical tone to much of this book, and the author seems to assume that money, not kinship, family, or even the act-consequence schema, does the most in determining whether things go well or ill for someone. Consider, for example, Ecclesiastes 5:8–14:

If you see the poor oppressed in a district, and justice and rights denied, do not be surprised by such things: for one official is eyed by a higher one, and over them both are others higher still. The increase from the land is taken by all; the king himself profits from the fields. Those who love money never have enough; those who love wealth are never satisfied with their income. This too is meaningless. As goods increase so too do those who consume them. And what benefit are they to the owners, except to feast their eyes on them? The sleep of laborers is sweet, whether they eat little or much, but the abundance of the rich permits them no sleep. I have seen an evil under the sun: wealth hoarded to the harm of its owners, or wealth lost through misfortune, so when they have children there is nothing left for them to inherit.

Clearly, we have here a very different set of assumptions about wealth than those we encounter in Proverbs. Far from wealth always being a sign of God's blessing, here we are talking about ill-gotten gains, the love of money (which is seen as a bad thing), greed. More possessions lead to more consumption, but not more real benefits. Indeed, in the situation of social dysfunction the wealthy do not sleep at all well at night, unlike those who have little to lose. Our author talks about the oppression of the poor through taxes and the tithing of crops. True, he does think that sometimes wealth and possessions can come from God, rather than from wickedness (Eccles. 5:19), but sometimes God withholds from wealthy people the ability to enjoy their wealth. Hence, Ecclesiastes 6:2 says, "God gives wealth, possessions and honor, so that people lack nothing their hearts desire, but God does not grant the ability to enjoy them, and a stranger enjoys them instead." The very next verse bemoans the fact that a person with possessions who can't enjoy his prosperity is worse off than a stillborn child!

Here we see the dark side, the problems that can come with wealth and prosperity—a sense of insecurity in a fallen world, an inability to enjoy what one has, the insatiable lust or greed for more. If we read Ecclesiastes 10 closely it appears that the rulers are spying on and ripping off the people, that the people do not trust their rulers, and that oppression is woven into the very fabric of the society. The society has degenerated to the point that it is every man for himself. The (unhappy) individualism so often noted in this book is caused in part by a breakdown in the social networks of trust between rulers and people, and between the rich and the poor.

It seems that our author is trying to correct various glib and superficial ways of viewing life from a sapiential (or wisdom-oriented) point
of view. He wants to say that the idea that hard work and true faith
always produces a prosperous life is not valid. He also wants to deny
that one can easily discern God's hand in life in a time of suffering
or oppression of various sorts. His basic insight is that while it is a
good thing to live wisely, doing so in dark times does not necessarily
lead to a happy, healthy, or prosperous life. In other words, virtue in
such a time must be its own reward, as it is otherwise inadequately
compensated.

A shadow of death hovers over this book in various places, and
sometimes death and Sheol cast a shadow of futility and absurdity
over all life's striving after prosperity or the good life. This leads the
sage to shrug his shoulders and suggest that one must, so to speak,
seize the day (9:10 and 11:9). It seems that the role of this book in the
Old Testament canon is to keep wisdom honest in a fallen world, by
encouraging a little honesty about the dark side of life.

What is of course missing here, as elsewhere in such early Wisdom
literature, is any sort of notion of an afterlife, or of reward or com-
pensation in the afterlife. It is safe to say that if the author believed
that there was a rectification of matters, especially of life's injustices
and evils, beyond the grave he would have looked at life differently
and not simply as vanity or meaninglessness. This is one of the main
differences between Jesus's wisdom teaching, which is also counter-
order wisdom, and that of Qoheleth. Jesus believes that after judgment
there will be a reversal of fortunes. Indeed, he believes that that reversal
is already beginning to happen through his ministry. A good example
of how Qoheleth can quote an old wisdom maxim, and then severely
qualify it, can be seen in Ecclesiastes 7:1: "A good name is better than
precious ointment" (something Solomon could have said), "and the
day of death better than the day of birth" (something the older mo-
narchial sages like Solomon would probably not have said).

More reflection on the relevant material in Ecclesiastes 5:10–20 is
in order. These verses attest to the fact that the author thinks that
wealth creates restlessness, not satisfaction or peace of mind in its
holders; that it brings no enduring benefit, and on the negative side
it attracts parasites; that it leads to sleeplessness and worry, whereas
the poor or day laborers sleep well at night; that there is no guarantee
it will provide security against an uncertain future—fortunes come
and then disappear quickly; and finally, that we can't take it with us

so we may as well try to enjoy it if we have it. Ecclesiastes 5:19–20 seems to suggest that there is no necessary positive correlation between industry and prosperity, between hard work and wealth. Wealth is rather a gift from God, and so is the ability to enjoy it, but God may withhold one or both of these things from a faithful person.

Clearly our author takes an independent approach to wisdom—sometimes he accepts conventional wisdom, sometimes he qualifies it, sometimes he rejects it. Notice the paradoxical nature of what the author says in Ecclesiastes 8:12–13: "Although a wicked person commits a hundred crimes and still lives a long time, I know that it will go better with God-fearing people, who are reverent before God. Yet because the wicked do not fear God, it will not go well with them, and their days will not lengthen like a shadow." It is entirely possible that Qoheleth is using a dialogical form of discourse here, meant to force the audience to reflect on the apparent contradictions in life. And so he may be saying that somewhere in this range of maxims lies the truth, not just in one or the other of them—and that much depends on the situation such a maxim addresses.

A close look at Ecclesiastes 8–9 confirms that our author does not think there is a necessary correlation between righteousness, longevity, and prosperity or, put another way, between health, wealth, and faithful living. While sometimes there is a connection between these things, it is not always so. And the reason it is sometimes not so is not a lack of faith, or even a lack of righteousness. Just how out of joint the times seem to Qoheleth is shown in Ecclesiastes 10:6–7: "Fools are put in many high positions, while the rich occupy the lower ones. I have seen slaves on horseback, while princes go on foot like slaves." The traditional status quo order presumed in Proverbs has broken down in Qoheleth's day. He does not endorse this state of affairs, but he does see it as a fact. What is most important about Ecclesiastes for our purposes is that it shows no naïveté about prosperity, or for that matter about wealth always being a divine gift rather than a result of oppression and greed. In light of Ecclesiastes, it thus becomes difficult to know how to respond to prosperity. If it comes from God then the advice is given to try to enjoy it, although our author would not say such a thing to one who has ill-gotten gains, obtained, for instance, by dishonesty. (It is a regular theme in Wisdom literature that dishonest business practices are never to be commended.) While Ecclesiastes looks like some of the teachings of Jesus on these subjects in regard to their counter-order and counterintuitive nature, Qoheleth offers no eschatology or hope that all will be set right in the end times. Jesus, on the other hand, does offer such hope.

And So?

In summary, if we are going to use the Old Testament teachings about wealth and prosperity, then we must use it all and not extract out of context only those sound bites that appeal to us. This means doing justice not only to what one finds in Proverbs in all its variety and paradoxes, but also to the even more challenging material in Ecclesiastes. In the latter book wealth and prosperity are not viewed as unequivocal goods, nor are they always the result of divine blessing. The concern over oppression of the poor by the rich and those in power is palpable here. Poverty is not a necessary sign of divine curse any more than wealth is a necessary sign of divine blessing, otherwise the appeals to help and alleviate poverty, especially when caused by oppression, are inexplicable.

As I stated in the first chapter, it is important for any Christian studying this material to bear in mind that it must not be taken in isolation from what the New Testament says on such topics. Furthermore, it must be remembered that, in any case, Christians are not under the regime of the old covenant after the advent of Christ. The standard for Christian moral behavior is different, and in some respects more demanding, than in the Old Testament. And the perspective on wealth and poverty, riches and money, and related subjects changes in light the eschatological character of the situation and the teaching of Jesus and his followers. A Christian theology of money, stewardship, wealth, prosperity, and/or health cannot at the end of the day be mainly based on Old Testament texts. But even if one were to base some of one's thinking on such texts, one would have to do justice to the variety of often paradoxical materials found in both Proverbs and Ecclesiastes.

3

Money in the Bartering World of Jesus

The holy passion of friendship is so sweet and steady and
loyal and enduring in nature that it will last through a whole
lifetime, if not asked to lend money.

—Mark Twain

One of the challenges that we, as modern readers of the Bible, have
to be aware of is anachronism. By that I mean the tendency we all
have to project modern ideas and circumstances back into the ancient
world of the Bible and its culture, which results in distortion or mis-
interpretation of the text. Notions about money and prosperity seem
to be especially susceptible to anachronism. Yet even a moment of
thoughtful reflection will tell us that, of course, the economic world
of antiquity was not identical to that in our world today, and the way
money functioned in the ancient world of Jesus must have been different from the role it plays today. To avoid anachronism as we begin
our study, we need to take a look at ancient economics and the way
markets and money worked in the world of Jesus and his disciples.

Ancient Economics: The World of Agriculture

The basis of all ancient economics was agriculture. This was true
before, during, and after the time of Jesus. Though we tend to think

43

in terms of the urban culture and city life that now dominate the landscape of the Western world, in antiquity most people worked on farms or in rural settings. The economy was not driven by stock markets, investment bankers, or banks in general. More than any other single factor, what controlled the economy was the weather. Famine and subsequent food shortages were almost routine occurrences in antiquity, regularly affecting the daily lives of most ancient peoples. In a world without refrigeration or grocery stores, prayers for rain and the desperate need for good crops were daily concerns that never let up.

The New Testament was written at a time when the Roman Empire had just begun. The ministry of Jesus in the late 20s AD did not take place until after the Roman Empire had control of the whole Mediterranean region, from Rome all the way to Egypt (and beyond). This means that the most fundamental reality to keep in mind is that the economy of that time period was not so much local but *global* in nature. Managed by Rome, this vast economy encompassed the entire Mediterranean Crescent, including all the lands of the Bible. Egypt was the ancient equivalent of our Kansas and the prairie farm states—the regional breadbasket where most of the wheat was produced. (This of course had been true for centuries, as the stories in Genesis about the hungry patriarchs going down to Egypt make clear.) There is a second major truth about the ancient economy that needs to be underscored: not only the agrarian affairs of ancient society, but also the social ends in general, including economic affairs, were controlled by very powerful elites. Thus, as D. E. Oakman puts it, "ancient economy was political economy."[1] Political control was all the more important since regular famines predictably generated considerable social unrest in affected regions.

In the Holy Land the season of rains came in the winter, followed by drought in the summer. Even today, there is hardly any rain in Israel between late May and late September. The lush vegetation one sees on tour in Israel is largely due to elaborate irrigation systems, not rainfall. Estimates of annual rainfall during ancient times run as low as fifty millimeters of rain in the Negev, due south of Israel, to as much as eight hundred millimeters in northern Galilee. This scarcity of natural moisture meant that the ancients used dry farming methods, which included only plowing up the topsoil so as to retain the moisture in the deeper soil below. The land of Israel was and is "a land of wheat and barley, of vines and fig trees and pomegranates, a land of olive trees and honey" (Deut. 8:8) because the farmers plant crops that grow quickly and are drought resistant. In this region grain, wine, olives, and figs were and are the staples of life (see Hos. 9:2–4; Prov. 9:5; Neh. 5:11).

According to this crop cycle grain would be harvested in late spring. Grapes were gathered in the summer and turned into juice. Olives were picked in the early fall. The sweet figs also came in the fall, not the spring. Only the less palatable, more bitter (though edible) male fruit was available in the spring. (Remember Jesus cursing the fig tree in the spring.) The grain crops were especially labor intensive, with predators to fend off and weeding that was required right up to the harvest.

Of course, raising crops was not the only way to provide food for one's family. The ancients were sheep and goat herders as well. Goat's milk, and the cheese produced from it, provided important dietary nutrients. It needs to be borne in mind that most ancient peoples did not regularly sacrifice animals for food. They could not afford to do so. They had a more vegetarian diet than most moderns. The temple economy in Jerusalem, however, depended on the offering of a large number of animals in sacrifice. So did the businessmen living in Bethlehem and the surrounding areas, who provided sheep and small birds for sacrifice.

In an age before grain combines and mechanical equipment, harvesting and processing crops were done entirely by animal labor and human hands. Most people lived in villages or rural areas and worked in agriculture. But there were a small number of elites who lived in cities, owned estates, and had the leisure to devote themselves to other pursuits, including education, religion, and politics. It seems clear that Oakman is right when he says "the finite surplus made possible by pre-industrial agriculture placed restraints on the absolute size of the elite. . . . Village economy in such empires was focused on domestic need and agriculture; urban economy was based on taxation of surplus and redistribution for elite ends."[2] Accordingly, the possibility of attaining real prosperity—much less wealth as we think of it today—was limited to a very small number of people.

Lacking our modern day malls and shops—before there were specialized businesses of any sort—village people made their own clothing, sandals, and tools, and typically built their own homes. There were, however, a few trades that a small number of people controlled. Examples of these would include the making of glass products (including drinking vessels), weapons, and fine furniture. Of course the minting of money was held in strict control by the elites. Money in antiquity was always produced and managed exclusively by the elite members of society, and was used by them for political and religious propaganda of various sorts. Money was "essentially an elite tool to facilitate tax collection or to aid elite-sponsored commerce."[3] So it is not an accident that almost the only time money comes up in the Jesus tradition is when there is a discussion of some sort of taxes, tolls, or contributions to the temple. Money was not the basis of the entire economy the way it is today. It was entirely possible for an ancient person to be prosperous and well-off while having little or no money at all, certainly no money invested in banks or temple treasuries. Furthermore, we know for a fact that a main reason there was such resistance to taxation in early Judaism was because of its economic impact. Many people had little left to feed their families once taxes were paid. It is interesting that although Jews historically had a very high view of work, including manual labor, the Greco-Roman elite attitude of disdain towards those who worked with their hands seems to have infiltrated elite Jewish culture even before Jesus's day (see Sir. 38:25–34).

Scholars of ancient economies often talk about the concept of limited good. In biblical culture there was both low productivity and no notable means of increasing productivity over time (as with, say, the help of modern fertilizers and modern irrigation techniques). Given these realities, ancient peoples tended to believe that the goods of life had been distributed, even distributed by God, and they could not be increased—they were decidedly "limited." This in turn meant that if a person wanted something he or she did not have, they had to barter for it (or steal it). It was not a matter of finding some way to make "more," in order to increase one's income and spending power. Under these pressures, and given the fact that droughts were regular and the land's fertility could become farmed-out and exhausted, many ancients expected frequent decreases in productivity, thus prosperity on a regular, cyclical basis.

Another factor affecting the economy of the ancient world was the honor-shame ideology. Poverty was not merely seen as unfortunate, it was seen as shameful. A person who was poor was a disgrace to society, possibly even blighted by God. The flip side of that attitude was that the wealthy were often viewed as the most honorable members of society, as those blessed by God. This was not always the case. Legislation and exhortations meant to protect the widow and orphan were not lacking in the Hebrew Scriptures (Exod. 22:22; Isa. 1:17), and this subject is taken up by Jesus and others as well. And we have already seen from the books of Proverbs and Ecclesiastes that the wicked wealthy were not an unknown group and could come under criticism (Prov. 22:16; 22:23; Eccles. 4:1–3). So we can accurately speak of a category of the pious poor that was also an exception to economic honor-shame ideology.

More Economic Realities in Jesus's Day

In addition to the honor-shame ideology and the factors that influenced agriculture and the production of crops, there were two other major economic realities that had an impact on the Holy Land during the time of Jesus. First, Judea was ruled directly by Rome through its procurators, and large estates run by absentee landlords controlled most of the economy. Tenant farming was the norm. And if it was not the landlord coming to collect taxes, it was the tax police who came to collect from these farmers in kind or in coin. It isn't by accident that estate managers, tax collectors, and slaves make a frequent appearance in the Gospels (Luke 12:42; 16:1–8; Mark 13:34–35).

Second, the situation in Galilee, with the corrupt and hardly pious client king Herod Antipas in charge, was not much better. (Note Luke's reference to Herod's having estates and estate managers in the region [Luke 8:1–3].) The oppression of the large estates meant that small farmers had difficulty making a living. Some were even reduced to becoming day laborers, having been pushed off the land altogether. In addition there were artisans, like Jesus—stonemasons, leatherworkers, woodworkers, and the like—who kept themselves solvent by working in some of Herod's major building schemes. One instance of this was the building of the new city Sepphoris, located only a stone's throw from Nazareth.

With all this said, we should not make the mistake of seeing the economic tensions in Jesus's culture as purely social in nature. It is important to bear in mind the long impact the theology of the Pentateuch had on the whole of Jewish culture. As Ekkehard and Wolfgang Stegemann say: "There is support for the idea that in this tradition a certain balance was achieved socioeconomically, especially between the interest of the peasants (for instance in the prohibition of interest and above all in the debt law with its remission of debt regulation) and those of the priests (for example, in the right to tax) and was elevated as sacred legal tradition."[4] Cultural norms and customs like the year of Jubilee, the prohibition of interest, care for widows and orphans—not to mention the basic theological notion of creation that the earth and all that is in it belongs to God—were certainly in play in Jesus's day. They shaped not only the way people thought about money and economic matters, but also their behavior.

For our purposes I must stress that Jesus speaks out of just such a theological orientation. For instance, in his inaugural sermon in his hometown synagogue, he announces that the year of Jubilee has arrived, setting free not only the slaves but the debt prisoners as well (Luke 4).[5] Jesus seems always to relate money matters to God matters. Of course he was not alone in this. The complaint about Jesus's disciples gleaning the grain from the edge of a field when hungry on the Sabbath is a complaint that recognizes the widespread right of the poor to do this, though presumably not on the Sabbath (see Mark 2:23–24).

One important economic factor we have not yet mentioned is fishing in the sea of Galilee. This provided an additional source of food and income. What we can say with some assurance is that in Jesus's era, the land around the sea of Galilee appears to have been rather fruitful, and the fishing trade as well. Josephus in fact emphasizes the productivity of Galilee and its fertile valleys.[6]

It is also important to emphasize the specific economic trends that were at work in Jesus's era. The Stegemanns stress that "Craft, business, and . . . trade flourished in the land of Israel, especially in connection with Hellenization [the spread of Greek culture], which also brought a certain urbanization. The spread of the coinage system which had already begun in the Persian [exilic] period also promoted trade. After this time, Palestine was also integrated economically into the eastern Mediterranean area and later into the broader area enclosed by the Roman empire. Handicrafts attained a certain specialization and differentiation."[7]

The need for artisans of various sorts in both Judea and Galilee was fueled by the enormously ambitious building projects of the Herods—including the building of the temple in Jerusalem, the Antonia Fortress, the Herodium, Caesarea by the Sea, Masada at the Dead Sea, the cities of Tiberias and Sepphoris in Galilee, and the rebuilding of Banyas, which became Caesarea Philippi, Herod Philip's capital city. Consider for a moment the enormous needs of a workforce in connection with the maintenance and activities of the temple in Jerusalem. Besides all the construction workers, the list of services needed is a long one: goldsmiths, silversmiths, shewbread bakers, producers of incense, sheep and small birds for sacrifice brought to Jerusalem from nearby sheep farms, keepers of the granary, treasurers, priests and Levites of various sorts, money changers, animal sellers, musicians, teachers, scribes, and lawyers.[8]

On the one hand Galilee was close to the old spice and north-south trade routes, including the so-called King's highway that ran from Petra up the rift valley passing to the east of the sea of Galilee. This brought products into the region that were not indigenous to Israel— iron, copper, lead, gold, silver, and, perhaps above all, spices. On the other hand southern Galilee was a good distance from the sea trade, and there was no port very close to this region (Joppa was too far for most Galileans). Crafts, business, and trade surely played a role in the Galilean economy, but they were subordinate to agriculture.

How exactly did the Herods pay for their enormous building projects? By levying taxes, and these on top of the levies Rome exacted. In addition, there were also toll collectors at the borders of the various regions. Jesus appears to have encountered both tax and toll collectors, and proselytized them. The Herods gobbled up the land, joining together small farms and turning them into large estates run by estate managers, slaves, and others. This transpired not only in Judea but also in Galilee. We can distinguish between royal estates owned by the Herods and the aristocratic estates owned by some of the other elites (including those in Judea), by Sadducees, and by priestly families such as that of Caiaphas.

As these realities suggest, the Herods simply regarded the whole land as their own territory. They assumed the right to confiscate a small farmer's land whenever desirable. Some of the newly created estates, as well as some of the long-standing ones already in operation, were enormous. For example, the estate that archaeologists have discovered near Shechem spanned over twenty-five hundred acres, involving a hundred and seventy-five or more families living on and farming the land. The process of confiscation turned small farmers into tenants on what had previously been their own land, or even day laborers. Estimates show that Herod himself garnered around a thousand talents annually in direct taxation, which makes it clear that the tax burden was high, especially when any of the Herods were involved in expensive building projects.[9] Confiscations made it impossible for farmers to be self-sufficient anymore, and they were reduced to working for the new estate owners, or even working on the building projects. It is no exaggeration to say that "the indebtedness of small farmers and the expropriation of their land are the hallmarks of this Roman epoch."[10] The steady decline of the little man from small farmer to tenant farmer to day laborer, even to outright begging, is unfortunately a major feature of this era, as was whole villages becoming dependent on the owner of one large estate. It is clearly not accidental that Jesus addresses the plight of day laborers and other dispossessed people in his parables.

Hillel, a famous Jewish teacher from just before the time of Jesus, through a legal fiction called the *prosbol* made it possible for a debt to be maintained even beyond a Jubilee year.[11] This was a most unfortunate gutting of the Jubilee legislation found in Deuteronomy 15, where a complete remission of debts was commanded. Jesus, had he known Hillel, would have rejected his approach altogether, as is apparent not only from Luke 4 but also from the Lord's prayer, which speaks about receiving forgiveness for debts just as one forgives others their debts. It may be that Hillel meant well, trying to enable the poor to obtain necessary loans, for while the Jubilee provision was considered law, moneylenders were reluctant to loan a poor person any money for survival. Be that as it may, the actual social effect of the *prosbol* benefited the loaners more than the debtors.

In a social situation where more and more persons were being pushed into poverty, it is not surprising that there arose a movement of zealots, beginning as early as AD 6 with Judas the Galilean. The zealots were prepared, if necessary, to use violence to retake the land for disenfranchised small farmers.

Taxing Situations in Jesus's Day

In order to fully understand the tax burden in Jesus's world, we need to bear in mind that there was a difference between religious taxes (such as the temple tax) and state or provincial taxes. Religious taxes included not only the temple tax referred to in the Gospels, but also the tithe and the firstlings tax. State taxes, on the other hand, included the head tax (hence the census referred to in Luke 2) and land taxes. There were also various sorts of sales taxes and taxes on goods, taxes on imports and exports, and tolls taken at borders. Then there was the ever popular practice of impressment, the involuntary drafting of a person to do a task, called *angaria* (see Matt. 5:41 and the example of Simon of Cyrene and the cross).

After the brief hiatus of the Maccabean era and the Hasomonean period, beginning in 37 BC Herod the Great once again instigated the practice of Jews paying tribute money to their overlords, in this case Caesar. This practice involved indirectly paying the tribute through the Herods, but in AD 6, when Archelaus lost his throne, the taxation became direct. This was the first occasion when Jews had to directly "render unto Caesar what is Caesar's." Tribute money had to be paid for every male family member fourteen years and older and every female twelve years and older, amounting to about one denarius per person per annum (Mark 12:13–17). This must not be confused with the temple tax, which Jews even in the Diaspora sent to the temple in Jerusalem. Jesus comments on both practices, as we shall see.

The Romans were notorious for getting other people to do their dirty work, and in the case of tax collecting this was a regular practice. Jews collected taxes from Jews for their Roman overlords. Notice, for example, the story in Luke 18:10–1, about the Jewish tax collector and the Pharisee in the temple. Notice as well the story in Luke 19 about a rich Jewish tax collector named Zaccheus for whom repentance meant giving back what he had extorted (for a start).

Not surprisingly, Jewish tax collectors were widely shunned and viewed as traitors because they collected taxes not just for the temple but for their oppressors. Many Jews thought the tribute money should not be paid at all, hence the question asked of Jesus about this matter (Mark 12:13–17). Tax farming was leased out to the highest bidder, and extortion was a normal practice, for the tax collector had to pay himself as well as the amount agreed upon with the lessors, the over-lords. It is clear that the tax burden was in many cases unbearable, with one estimate suggesting that the "federal" tax amounted to as much as three denarii per person (on top of the religious taxes). A denarius was about the equivalent of one day's pay for a day laborer, who made only a subsistence wage, so three denarii was an exorbitant tax. While we are not sure exactly when the temple tax was imposed on Jews, it was certainly before the time of Jesus, and probably as early as the Hasmonean period (140–137 BC).[12]

How was the Jerusalem temple tax paid? It did not involve everyone traveling to Jerusalem and dropping money in the temple treasury. The

Jewish writer Philo tells us that holy funds were gathered by respected members of a village or town and put in a town treasury. Then reliable emissaries were sent to Jerusalem to pay the tax.[13] It appears likely that these emissaries traveled to Jerusalem during festival seasons, so they could travel with pilgrims going to celebrate Passover or other feasts. (There was safety in numbers.)

The money for the temple tax was considered holy money, not least because it paid for the sacrifice of atonement year after year. The coin of choice for this temple tax was the Tyrian half-shekel because it was made of pure silver and had a constant weight (see below). The fact that it had a picture of Herakles (Hercules) and the Ptolemaic eagle on it apparently was not much of a deterrent to using such coins for a sacred purpose. It appears to have been an innovation in Jesus's own era to have money changers and animal sales right in the temple precincts whereas previously they had been outside. Jesus saw this as a form of defilement, especially if it involved unfair trading within the boundaries of the holy place.

Perhaps equally onerous, and not much discussed in the work of New Testament scholars, were the tithes paid to the priests (a tenth; see Num. 18:21–32 and Neh. 10:38 on the postexilic practice; cf. *Jubilees* 13:24ff.). Josephus says that he knew of priests who got rich from collecting these tithes.[14] One wonders if the lawyers who bilked widows, about which Jesus specifically complained, were working for such priests (see below).

Enough has now been said to provide a general picture of the monetary and economic situation in the Holy Land during the time of Jesus. It is not a rosy picture, except for some of the elites. This is the social context in which Jesus's comments about money and wealth must be considered. In that era, wealth and extensive property more often than not were associated with graft, corruption, and extortion rather than God's blessings. And money, with pictures of pagan rulers or Greek heroes on it, was not seen as a morally neutral resource. We now need to talk more particularly about the coins of that era.

Coins of the Realm

Over many years I have collected various first-century coins mentioned in the New Testament. I'll describe them for you here. The first and largest of these coins is the Tyrian shekel (minted in Tyre), with a picture of Herakles (Hercules) on one side and the eagle of the Ptolemys (successors to Alexander in Egypt) on the other. The Tyrian half-shekel was literally half the size and weight of the shekel. Here we note that precious metals were used in transactions even before coins were minted, and the way trades were made was on the basis of the weight of the precious metal. This concern about weight carried over into the process of evaluating the worth of coins. Both the type of metal and its weight counted in such matters. It was these coins that were taken to the temple in Jerusalem for the payment of the temple tax.

Another coin made of silver was the silver denarius, which regularly had the head of one or another emperor on it. The two examples I have show the images of Augustus and Nero. Most Jews considered these coins to have graven images on them, not least because these coins mentioned that the emperor was the son or descendant of the divine, or divinized, Augustus. These were the coins normally used to pay the tribute to Rome, and it is indeed these coins that Jesus was asked to make a judgment about (Matt. 17:24–27). The obverse side of the coin could have a variety of images. The Augustus coin has his two nephews Caius and Lucius on the back, whereas the Nero coin has a temple. (It is probably the Nero coin's inscription which speaks of "Nero Caesar the divine son of Augustus" that is the basis of the symbolic number 666. Numerical values were assigned to each of the letters of the Greek and Latin and Hebrew alphabets and when this inscription's numerical values are "added up" we get to 666, and also the variant "616" found in some texts of Rev. 13:17–18, depending on which language's text you are adding up.)

The next coin, which was worth far less than the ones mentioned thus far, is the lepta or so-called widow's mite. It is coins like this that Jesus saw a woman throw into the temple treasury in Jerusalem (Mark 12:41–44). It is interesting that an indigent widow would have coins at all, but perhaps not so surprising that any coins she did have were of such low value, worth less than a modern penny. Like our penny, the lepta was a copper coin. And the lepta, like other coins minted by Jews, did not have human images on them. Mine has a wheel or rosette-like image on one side and a lamp on the other.

The next coins of interest to us are the procurator coins, first the Pontius Pilate coin, then the Festus coin, and finally the Felix coin. The Pilate coin, like the Felix, was made of bronze, as was typical of such coins actually minted in Judea. It features an olive branch on one side and the shepherd's crook, an emblem of leadership, on the other. As we have noted, coins were a major means of propaganda. This coin is meant to symbolize that Rome's governors come in peace and will be beneficent leaders. (Alas, that was seldom so!) The Felix coin is even more interesting. It has a fruit-bearing palm tree on one side, and on the other the Roman fiscus, the symbol of Roman justice. The Felix coin is important as it helps us date the reign of Felix and Festus, since Claudius the emperor died in AD 54, and he is mentioned on the fiscus side of the coin.

Herod the Great minted his own coins, which is not surprising since he fancied himself a ruler in the mold of the great Hellenistic leaders. His coins did not have images on them, and they do not show the degree of artisanship and skill that other coins of the era do. It is not an accident that the temple in Jerusalem, even during Herod's lifetime, preferred the temple tax to be paid in Tyrian shekels. The shekels were the gold standard (or, more strictly speaking in this case, the silver standard) of coins in the region. Herod ruled for a very long time, from 37 BC until his death in about 2 BC, so there are plenty of his coins around. But Herod chose to leave his legacy primarily in his buildings, not his coins. This may suggest that he had more sense than the procurators when it came to the Jewish sensibilities of his subjects, at least in some ways. Herod of course was not a pure Jew, he was also Idumean, which made him objectionable to many Jews but perhaps less so than being a Roman.[15]

In summary, let me reiterate a few key points about economics in the NT world:

1. *The ancient economy was not a money economy*, and money was mainly used to pay taxes, tolls, tribute. It could also be used for a dowry (see the parable of the lost coin, and the story about the widow's mite).

2. *There was no free market capitalism in Jesus's world.* What decided financial issues—when it came to imposing taxes, fixing labor costs, and the like—was usually whatever the elites wanted to do. Bartering was still normal, and was affected by things like patron-client relationships. In other words, there was no such thing as money as a great equalizer in this world. Social status and standing determined what sort of economic transactions one could undertake. Land, and the social standing that came with having land, was more important

than possessing coinage, especially in a small country with a scarce supply of arable and fertile soil.

3. *Money had explicit religious connotations in antiquity* that it seldom does today. In the social world of Jesus, political, social, economic and religious matters were all intertwined.

4. *Religious values affected how one viewed property, money, and prosperity*, and undergirding Jewish views was the belief in a single creator God to whom all things ultimately belonged.

5. *By Jesus's day there had been a long history of Jews not ruling their own country*, and a long history of oppression, even in the Holy Land. Thus the attainment of wealth was often a matter of collusion with the oppressors of your own people. Gone were the days when wealth was simply assumed to be a blessing from God, no matter who had the wealth or was prosperous. Wealth might be a blessing from God, but it might also be as a sign of graft and wickedness.

The Social World of Jesus

As we close this chapter and turn to Jesus's views on money, property, and prosperity we need to make a few additional, orienting comments about the society in which Jesus lived. First note that, with the exception of some royal or elite persons, money and property were overwhelmingly in the hands of men. There were all sorts of gender-based double standards in Jesus's culture, including ownership of property. It was a widespread view of many early Jews that women were not entitled to own property.[16] Also in terms of gender relations, women and men had very different roles. Women were expected to raise the family, take care of the house, and perhaps help with some aspect of the farming. Men were the public face of the family, dealing with other men when it came to bartering for goods, dealing with tax collectors, negotiating with the elders in the village, and so forth. Since Jesus does not always honor these distinctions, what he says about money, resources, honoring parents, and the like often goes against the social conventions of his culture.

Second, Jesus lived in a volatile age. Judea had been taken over by the procurator Pontius Pilate in AD 26. Pilate had committed a string of offenses against the religious sensibilities of the Jews, including an attempt to place Roman standards with their eagles atop in the holy place in Jerusalem (cf. Luke 13:1). He was not to be trusted. Jesus thought even less of Herod Antipas, the executor of his cousin John the Baptizer and the one he dubbed "that fox" (see Luke 13:32). Thus Jesus's remarks about property, prosperity, and money must be understood in the context of an *adversarial situation*, where there were already Jews prepared to use violence against their oppressors—the bilkers, the extortioners, the tax collectors, and the rulers.

Third, it should go without saying that Jesus was a profoundly religious person. His religious commitments took him to Jerusalem on various occasions, even when it was dangerous, and these commitments strongly conditioned what he said about money and possessions. For example, his view that God's kingdom was beginning with his ministry strongly colored his wisdom about material things, about what amounts to a truly good life, and what one should do with one's property. We need look no further than the story where Jesus tells a young man to sell all he has, give to the poor, and come follow him, to understand the great extent to which Jesus's views of money and property were affected by his religious commitments.

And now we are ready to undertake an extended discussion of what those views were.

4

Jesus and the Treasure Hunt

Never work just for money or for power. They won't save
your soul or help you sleep at night.

—Marian Wright Edelman

It is perhaps one of the greatest tragic ironies imaginable that the
teaching of Jesus has been used by affluent modern Christians to justify
the lifestyles of the rich and famous. This is the very same Jesus who
said "blessed are the poor" and warned "do not store up treasures
on earth." Simple phrases like "you have not because you ask not" or
"ask (in faith) and you shall receive" have been turned into mantras
that are thought to produce nearly instant material benefits. In light
of the persistence of a distorted prosperity gospel, and in light of
the economic downturn we all face, now is a good time to visit anew
the teachings of Jesus on the subject of money. While we are at it,
it seems appropriate to ask, What was Jesus's lifestyle like? Was he
a wealthy man, as some prosperity preachers have insisted? Or was
he a peasant as some biblical scholars have claimed? Was he neither?
Inquiring minds want to know.

Jesus on the Money

In a world where there was no separation of religion and state, Mark
12:13–17 takes on a very different look than it often does in the mod-

ern Western world, increasingly preoccupied with the separation of church and state. Here Jesus is asked, "Is it lawful to pay taxes to the emperor, or not?" It is altogether believable that Jesus would be questioned about the issue of tribute money to Caesar in the volatile milieu of the Holy Land, where violent revolutionaries and zealots continually argued that there should be no cooperation with their oppressive overlords.

The coin in question in this remarkable discussion, meant to test Jesus's mettle so to speak, is probably the second series of denarii issued by the Emperor Tiberius. It reads on one side PONTIF MAXIM (making it clear that the Emperor himself was the high priest of Roman religion) and on the other side TI CAESAR DIVI FILII AVGVSTVS, that is, Caesar and son of the divine Augustus. For many early Jews even possessing such a coin, whether to pay the tribute to Caesar or for some other purpose, amounted to recognizing the claims Caesar was making on the coin to be both high priest and son of the divine Augustus. This in turn was seen as a fundamental betrayal of monotheism and the Jewish religion in general.

The probable setting for this discussion was Judea, which was ruled directly by Rome. It was here that the Romans or their underlings collected the tribute money without intermediaries such as client kings. It may well be that this discussion took place during Jesus's final visit to Jerusalem, when many were trying to trap him in his words, and so find an excuse to remove him from the scene. We must bear in mind that already in AD 6 the zealot Judas the Galilean had established the principle that it was sacrilegious and immoral to pay the tribute money. This little story in Mark (also found in Matt. 22:15–22 and Luke 20:20–26), then, is probably meant to reveal how Jesus's views *differed* from those of the zealots. One word of caution is in order. The fact that Jesus was not a violent revolutionary doesn't mean that he was socially conservative and thus not a threat to the status quo. In fact, Jesus was socially quite radical in a number of ways, for example, in his views of women and their roles.[1] The question here, however, is his view of the tribute money.[2]

The query posed to Jesus requests an opinion concerning the legality of paying the tribute. The phrase "is it permitted" alludes to permission given in the Mosaic law (cf. Mark 3:4; 1 Cor. 14:34). Jesus's response depends on the assumption that the person who mints the coins and has his picture on them is the one to whom they belong. Here it is helpful to note that there are several Gospel texts that suggest that

Jesus did not have much regard for "money" as it existed in his day. For example, Matthew 6:24 says that one cannot be a servant or slave of both God and mammon (i.e., money). Luke 16:9 is more pointed, calling money "unrighteous mammon." (This is perhaps where we get colloquial phrases such as "filthy lucre.") There are also the texts where Jesus sees money or wealth in general as an obstacle to entering the kingdom of God that is breaking into the world through Jesus's life and ministry. In this connection, the story of the rich young ruler comes to mind, with its closing aphorism, "It is easier for a camel to go through the eye of a needle than for a rich man to enter God's kingdom" (Mark 10:25). We may think as well of the parable of the rich man and Lazarus, in which the rich man ends up in Hades and poor Lazarus in Abraham's bosom in heaven (Luke 16:19–31). In light of these other passages, it is hardly likely that Jesus's advice to "render to Caesar what is Caesar's" was intended to indicate that a Jew should be civic-minded and pay his taxes, though this saying has often been read that way.

Furthermore, this saying has nothing to do with modern theories about two spheres of influence, the secular and sacred realms, with appropriate duties owed in each by the believing person. Rather than being a counsel of submission to earthly rulers, Mark 12:13–17 is more likely a comment on the relative insignificance of the coin or taxes, in light of the fact that Jesus himself is now bringing God's saving reign upon the earth.

Notice that Jesus has no such coin on his person, but his inquisitors do. This would have been viewed as a plus for Jesus if there were any budding revolutionaries in the audience. To carry such coins was to traffic in graven images, in the minds of many devout Jews. Jesus certainly did not approve of idolatry, and it is understandable how using such coins, in view of their images and inscriptions, could be seen as idolatrous. It is fair to say, however, that the way Jesus responds to the question would likely have been seen by revolutionaries as a deplorable compromise with the powers that be.

Herein lies a major difference between Jesus and the revolutionaries. Jesus believed that God's reign in the Holy Land was being established by him and his disciples through preaching, teaching, and healing, whereas the revolutionaries thought that the way forward necessarily involved the violent overthrow of Caesar's puppets and representatives. Jesus was a theocrat, not a bureaucrat or a revolutionary. By this I mean that he believed God was directly intervening to set things

right through his ministry, and neither conflict with government authorities nor actual compromise with them was a denial or betrayal
of the saving activity that was occurring without the aid of politics
or plotting. Whether one paid the tribute money to Caesar or not,
this neither helped nor hindered the coming of the kingdom on earth.
God's divine intervention was bigger and more powerful than any
sort of human social arrangements or machinations.

In short, Jesus disagreed that the paying of the tribute was a litmus
test that determined one's loyalty or disloyalty to the biblical God.
In fact, giving Caesar back his meaningless pieces of metal that bore
his image could be seen as a religious duty, for this sort of "return
to sender" implies a refusal to have anything to do with things that
Caesar has made or minted. What is especially interesting about the
way Jesus eludes the trap that was set for him (compare John 7:53–
8:11) is that his response would neither satisfy the revolutionaries
nor give the Herodians or Pharisees reason to turn him over to the
Roman authorities. This saying could not be seen as seditious, and
it is probable that Jesus intended it to be something of a riddle or
brainteaser, as was typical of the way early Jewish sages responded
in such tight spots.

If the coin is Caesar's, what then should we render back to God?
Jesus does not say here, but it is unlikely that he is suddenly referring to paying the temple tax, having been discussing the other
major money issue—the tribute money. It is more likely that Jesus
is concerned with ultimate issues and the giving of one's whole self
to God. Jesus certainly had a clear creation theology that informs
many of his views (see how it informs his theology of marriage in
Mark 10). It is even possible that we should see here a subtle contrast
between the image on the coin and human beings created in the
image of God. Now, in view of the in-breaking of God's kingdom,
it is time for all persons created in God's image to give their whole
selves to God because—just as Caesar claimed to own all coins with
his image—so God claims ownership over all creatures that bear his
image. Now is the time to render God his proper due. The response
of the crowd to Jesus's distinctive teaching is not unexpected. They
have never heard this sort of wisdom before, and they are puzzled
by it.

Our next text, Matthew 17:24–27, deals with the issue of the temple
tax itself. In this story Peter is asked if Jesus pays the temple tax. Peter
answers that he does, and when he later discusses this with Jesus he is

told to go fishing—a coin to pay the tax will be found in the mouth of the first fish caught. This story is found only in Matthew, and we can well imagine why a tax collector like Matthew would have an interest in this subject. One of the issues that is often overlooked in this text is that Jesus lives in an honor and shame culture, where persons often did things so as not to shame those to whom they were close. It is not clear that Jesus heartily endorses the temple tax in this passage, but on the other hand, he does not flatly refuse to pay it, either.

We have already spoken briefly about the Tyrian shekel and half shekel in the last chapter, but here a few more pertinent facts can be added. These sorts of coins were minted in Tyre from about 126 BC to about AD 56, thus including the entire span of Jesus's life. These were the coins of choice for important purposes, and since they came to be used for the temple tax, they were even treated as sacred money. This was the case in spite of the image of Herakles on them, and in spite of the inscription "Tyre the holy and invincible," an odd inscription for a coin that kept ending up in the precincts of the Jewish temple in Jerusalem. (Note, though, that these coins would be exchanged by the money changers for coins that could be placed directly into the temple treasury without defilement or sacrilege.)

It is quite possible that one reason Jesus objected to what the money changers were doing in the outer courts of the temple is that it involved these pagan coins. The coin was in wide circulation throughout Galilee, Samaria, and Judea, and could readily be found in a place like Capernaum. Tyre was close by, and Jesus even visited the region of Tyre on one occasion (see Mark 7:24–30). He surely must have known all about this coin, its images and inscriptions. Furthermore, the Tyrian shekels were plentiful enough that it is not hard to imagine some of these coins turning up around the Sea of Galilee, since toll and tax collectors sometimes traveled by boat across the lake, as did businesspersons who were involved in the fish trade.[3]

The temple tax (also known as the two-drachma tax) was normally collected in the spring, more particularly in March before the Passover.[4] Thus the setting of this story, the final journey up to Jerusalem to the temple made by Jesus and his disciples in late March or early April in AD 30, makes perfect sense. The inquiry here comes from tax collectors, not from Pharisees or Sadducees, and it is very remarkable that Jesus goes out of his way not to offend these tax collectors. Jesus appears here as a pious and loyal Jew, even though he seems to think he is exempt from, or not required to pay, this tax.

Notice how the story begins with Peter affirming that Jesus does indeed pay the tax. In this Gospel this story comes before the "render unto Caesar" story and provides the first glimpse in Matthew of Jesus's views on taxes of any sort. It is probably the case that this story was important for the evangelist and his audience of Jewish Christians in Galilee, even sometime after AD 70 when the temple was destroyed.

The story opens in Matthew 17:24 with the disciples coming back home to Capernaum before the final trip to Jerusalem. The tax collectors come and ask their question negatively: "Doesn't your master pay the temple tax?" The probable reason for framing the question this way is that there was some resistance to paying the tax in Galilee, as some Galileans thought the temple was corrupt. It is interesting that the Qumran community (i.e., the Dead Sea sectarians) refused to pay this tax annually, but they did pay it once in a lifetime.[5] The basis for this tax—the half-shekel tax on all adult males to "atone for your lives"—is actually in the law (Exod. 30:13–16).

Note how in Jesus's reply he implies that he (and presumably his disciples) are children of the great King, and as such should be exempt from a tax levied by the temple, thus ultimately by God. Jesus here is drawing on the well-known practice in the Mediterranean world of kings exempting their own children from taxation. So Jesus's response is not totally unprecedented and is within the parameters of what might be legally debated about the matter after AD 70.

Verse 25 depicts Jesus as a prophetic sage who knows what Peter has been discussing before Peter speaks to him, and so he speaks first as he enters the house: "What do you think, Simon—from whom do kings of the earth collect duty and taxes, from their own sons, or from others?" When Peter replies "from others," Jesus presses the conclusion: "So then the sons are free [i.e., exempt, free not to pay]." In this context, the others that Jesus and Peter refer to must be Jews who are not followers of Jesus, because the temple tax was not collected from non-Jews, even if they lived in the Holy Land. But notice as well that Jesus says "sons," using the plural. He is thus not just talking about a personal exemption as the Son of God from such a tax, but in fact an exemption for both himself and his followers. The disciples are not obligated to pay a tax to their heavenly Father (cf. Matt. 5:16, 48; 6:1; 23:9). This teaching shows Jesus's radical nature. He feels free to declare not only who is and is not a son of the King, but also who does and does not have an obligation to pay this tax. Jesus's actions here reveal the sovereign and free way he relates to the Mosaic law, declaring that parts of it are not obligatory for himself or his followers. (The whole idea of a temple tax is of course interesting for Americans and others who are used to churches being tax-exempt.)

Jesus believes that new rules apply, now that the kingdom of God is breaking into human history. In light of what has come before, verse 27 provides a surprising conclusion to the story. It could have ended with Jesus simply saying "we're not paying," or he could have asked that the tax be paid out of the disciples' common money bag. Instead, Jesus does not want to unnecessarily offend the tax collectors, so he tells Peter: "Go fishing!"

But that is not all. Jesus tells Peter to take the first fish he finds, open its mouth, and he will find the Tyrian shekel in the fish—enough to pay both his own and Peter's temple tax. So Jesus does not object to paying the temple tax, but he thinks the children of the King are not *required* to do so. Clearly Jesus is envisioning a miracle or a unique providence of God here, and perhaps this is the only miracle Jesus spoke of that has a direct personal benefit for himself and a disciple but no one else.

But notice that the story does not end by relating that Peter actually goes fishing and finds a coin. It's possible that Jesus was joking, and if so this would be an example of a sage's wry sense of humor. It's hard to doubt, however, that this story would have been forgotten and never passed down in the Gospel if in fact the outcome had been different from what Jesus predicted. It is significant that the only time Jesus directly discusses money is either in the context of a discussion of taxes, or when he uses the broader terms *mammon* or *unrighteous mammon*. Clearly enough, he does not have a very high view of money. Or, better said, he does not have a very high view of the effect money has on most fallen human beings.

To sum up, how then does Jesus feel about taxes and taxation? On the one hand, we do not find him giving long exhortations to pay taxes and so fulfill one's civic duty. Yet on the other hand, he does not object to the principle of paying taxes, though he considers himself and his followers to be exempt (as children of the greatest king, God). This same saying susggests that Jesus thought his followers were exempt from the Old Testament requirement to tithe to the Temple. The "render unto Caesar" clause could be interpreted to imply that it was even all right to pay taxes to the Roman emperor, which seems to be the way some of Jesus's earliest followers understood his teaching on the matter.[6] We now turn to the broader subjects of amassing wealth, storing up treasure, and getting rich.

Jesus on Storing Up Treasures on Earth

While parables and other metaphorical teachings of Jesus can sometimes be rather cryptic, at other times their meaning is so obvious
and jarring that they feel like a slap in the face. One such saying is
found in the Sermon on the Mount (Matt. 6:19–21). Here a literal
translation of the Greek is in order: "Do not treasure up treasures on
earth, where moths and eaters can consume [or destroy], and thieves
can dig through the house wall [or the wall of the temple treasury,
where valuables were often put on deposit] and steal. Rather treasure
up treasure in heaven, where these things cannot happen. For where
your treasure is, there also is your heart."

The heart in Semitic ways of thinking was the control center of the
human personality—the center of thought, feelings, and will. This
parable is suggesting that whatever one counts as treasure, whatever
one values most, will determine one's life orientation—what one will
do with one's time, money, and other resources. One's treasure is the
ultimate expression of one's person or character. Thus the point here
is not so much to seek better treasures (rewards in heaven, though
Jesus does talk about such things), but to place one's allegiance with
God and God's priorities. This makes perfectly good sense in light
of what precedes this text: Jesus tells his listeners not to worry about
what they are to eat or drink, for God knows our needs. Seek first the
kingdom of God, and other things will be added.

We can make at least two mistakes in interpreting this passage.
One mistake is to overly spiritualize this teaching, as if it has only
to do with hidden matters of the heart and is of no relevance for
our discussion of what we should do with our material, physical
resources. The other mistake is to assume that if we first just seek
God's kingdom, then God will lavish all the material things we could
want upon us. To avoid these mistakes, we need to consider the parallel text in Luke 12.

But before we do this, we should be clear that Jesus in Matthew
6:25–34 has been talking about God providing the basic necessities
of life for his followers, not wealth or riches. It is *daily* bread that
believers are urged to pray for earlier in Matthew 6. Bearing these
things in mind, we turn now to Luke 12:29–34:

> And do not set your heart on what you will eat or drink; do not worry
> about it. For the pagan world runs after all such things, and your Father

knows you need them. But seek his kingdom, and these things [the necessities of food, drink, clothing just described] will be given to you as well. Do not be afraid, little flock, for your Father has been pleased to give you the kingdom. Sell your possessions and give to the poor. Provide purses for yourselves that will not wear out, a treasure in heaven that will not be exhausted, where no thief comes near and no moth destroys. For where your treasure is, there your heart will be also.

Clearly the passage in Luke is a variant of the one in Matthew, with Luke providing a practical example of what can be done on earth to store up treasures in heaven—namely, sell one's possessions and give to the poor. This of course is not the version of this teaching that one will hear a prosperity preacher citing. In fact, Luke has enormous concern about the effects of wealth on a believer's life, and is equally concerned for the poor.

In 12:30 Luke says that it is the nations of the world who are characterized by worry over the necessities of life (cf. Matt. 6:25). This is presumably in contrast to what should characterize the people of God. This reference to the Gentiles is probably another telltale sign about the ethnic extraction of Luke's audience. There are two variations in verse 31 from the Matthean parallel (Matt. 6:33). Luke says that disciples are simply to seek the kingdom; there is no reference to "first," as in Matthew. This suggests that it is the only real priority (cf. Luke 10:38–42). Luke omits "and its righteousness." What Jesus suggests is that if one gives up the search or striving for material things, at least the necessities will be provided as one seek the kingdom.

Luke 12:32 reassures the disciple that it is God's intention—indeed it is God's delight—to give his followers the kingdom, so one should not think of this as an impossible dream or an arduous and futile search for paradise. Like God, disciples are to be generous: they are to sell their possessions[7] (it does not say all of them) and give alms to the poor. By doing this they are storing up treasures in heaven. The idea here is that doing such things will be reckoned to their eternal credit. There may also be implied the idea of rewards in heaven.[8]

Verse 34 is an important aphorism of Jesus that suggests that one will set one's heart on whatever one most values. Instead of setting your heart on material possessions, you should set your heart on God and his kingdom above all other treasures. As Craig Evans notes, "People put their time, energies, and resources into those things they value, those things dear to their heart. Resources invested in material things are a sure sign that the things of this world are valued and not the things of God's kingdom."[9]

It's appropriate here to look at the parable of the rich fool who built bigger and bigger barns (Luke 12:16–21). The parable in verses 16–20 is meant to make clear the foolishness of the sort of reasoning that says, "If I can just have a few more good crops or returns on investment, then I will be financially secure and retire early and live the high life." As we have seen in an earlier chapter on Proverbs, Wisdom literature is full of contrasts between the wise and the foolish, and it needs to be stressed that the stock figure of the fool is not the ignoramus or mentally challenged person. Fools are the self-referenced and self-centered persons who think they run their own life and world, failing to take into account God, God's will, and God's word. Fools may well be smart or even savvy about some things. But they are not wise, they are not spiritually or morally discerning about the real nature of life and reality. In particular, they hardly ever factor in the uncertainty of the timing of their own demise.

The fact that this is a uniquely Lukan parable shows just how concerned Luke is with the issue of what we do with our possessions. Notice that the abundant crop of the rich fool never causes him to consider that maybe he now has an opportunity to help those in need (cf. Luke 16:19–25). The only thought a bigger crop prompts for him is that he needs to tear down present storage facilities and build larger ones. But suddenly death intervenes. The man's life is taken from him, bringing all his grandiose self-centered plans to naught. Verse 21 brings home the application: this parable illustrates how life goes for those who "make a treasure for themselves" but are not "rich towards God." As Luke Timothy Johnson observes, "Wealth with respect to God has two levels of meaning for Luke: the first is the response of faith, the second is the disposition of possessions in accordance with faith, which means to share them with others rather than accumulating them for one's self (see 16:9–13)."[10]

And here it begins to become clear that Jesus is all in favor of a person being rich—rich towards God that is, and generous towards one's fellow human beings, especially the poor. *What Jesus is not at all keen on is persons who are all about enhancing their own assets, portfolios, standards of living, or retirement accounts*, which in one sense is what the rich fool envisioned. Jesus has only warnings for rich fools, warnings about the danger of unrighteous mammon.

Mammon is the Aramaic word for riches. Jesus puts a human face on the term; thus he speaks about mammon as a master of persons, a master that one must forsake if one wishes to be a servant of God. But in the parable of the wicked servant (Luke 16) we learn more about Jesus's views on these matters, so we should consider it in some depth. We will need some extra help from the commentators with this parable because there is much debate in regard to what it is really telling us about God and the behavior of believers. Some even use this parable to justify business practices that are less than fully honest.

Luke 16:1 makes clear from the outset that the teaching in this chapter is for disciples of Jesus. The scenario set up in verse 2 is that a rich man has an estate manager, whom someone has charged with squandering the man's property. That this is not a false allegation seems clear from verse 8, where the manager is called dishonest. It is possible that something is going on in this parable that is not apparent on the surface. The rich man has various people in his debt.

We are not told if the rich man offered his loans with or without interest. But in view of the rich man's admiration for his manager's shrewdness, we may suspect that he had made loans with interest. J. D. M. Derrett has suggested that what the manager did was forego the interest involved and get the debtors to pay off the principle.[11] Of course there were various texts in the Hebrew Scriptures that warned against usury (cf. Deut. 15:7–8; 23:20–21; Exod. 22:24; Lev. 23:36–37). So possibly the manager does something biblical for a change, treating the debtors according to biblical principles, and thereby winning friends among them, friends who might be needed if he is indeed fired. Joseph Fitzmyer varies this approach by suggesting that what the manager does is subtract the commission on the goods and collect the principle.[12]

Concerning Derrett's suggestion, we might speculate that there was a variable rate of interest charged, since one person ends up paying 50 percent of what he originally owes and the other 80 percent. This too is possible, since interest was sometimes charged according to what the lender may have thought the person could eventually afford to pay.

In regard to Fitzmyer's suggestion, notice that the manager has to ask the debtors what they owe. Would it really be the case that he doesn't already know the amount if he originally brokered the deal and has a commission riding on the debt? That seems unlikely. What the owner asked for was to see the manager's records or accounts, or to hear a report about them (v. 2). It appears that the manager's job is to manage the estate, not to lend things without the owner's initiative. This means the manager is not the original lender and is not working on commission. He is a hired hand. The debt was owed directly to the rich man with interest, and the manager was only a collection agency.

The desperation of the manager is clear. He has learned that he is without a job, so he acts desperately to secure his future by making friends with those who might be his future employers. We get a glimpse into the manager's state of mind in verses 3–4. He admits to himself that he is not strong enough to do manual labor (like digging) and he's too proud—or better said—too ashamed to beg. Thus he devises a strategy to be welcomed into the homes of persons who will likely be grateful for his help with debt relief—and perhaps even give him a job.

One man owes a hundred jugs of olive oil, another a hundred containers of wheat. The debts are clearly owed to the master, not to the manager who acts as the middleman (see v. 5: "how much do you owe my master?"). Notice also the reference in verse 6 to paying the bill quickly. This is not a bartering situation. The debtor is presented with a bill and expected to pay in coin, not in kind. The going rate for a hundred baths of oil was about a thousand denarii, or just over three years' wages for a day laborer. The going rate for the hundred containers of wheat (perhaps about a thousand bushels) was about twenty-five hundred to three thousand denarii, or about eight to nine years' wages, a substantial sum indeed.

When we get to verse 8 we are told that the manager is not only dishonest but shrewd. Presumably this means he was formerly dishonest, since reducing the debtors' burdens is not in itself dishonest. Had this particular transaction been dishonest, the owner should have been at least a little upset. Verse 8 also suggests that there is something to be learned from the behavior of this steward, in that we are told that the children of this age are shrewder in dealing with their own kind than are the children of light. What exactly is the lesson the disciples are to learn here?

Verse 9 says that the lesson has to do with making friends by means of reducing someone else's debt, so that one will be welcomed into eternal tents. More precisely, what the text advises is to make friends by means of unrighteous mammon. This phrase seems to refer to the fact that there is an alluring quality to money that prompts humans, especially greedy ones, to act in unrighteous ways. Had Jesus thought that money is inherently and altogether evil he wouldn't be teaching lessons about its proper and improper uses. What this parable seems to teach is that the disciples should be opportunistic and generous to "debtors," and there will be reward in the eternal habitations if one behaves in that fashion. In other words, it teaches the same lesson as Luke 12:33. As Craig Evans comments, "Jesus is not recommending compromise and he is certainly not recommending dishonesty, but he is urging his followers not to overlook opportunities and resources that will sustain his people and advance the . . . mission."[13]

The saying in verses 10–11 ("Whoever is faithful in a little is also faithful in much") seems to follow from the parable rather well. Here we also get a clearer picture of Jesus's view of money in the contrast between true wealth and unrighteous mammon. Jesus apparently means that money is not true wealth, and money is inherently tainted; there is too much temptation for most fallen human beings to use it dishonestly. We also have here a "from the lesser to the greater" sort of argument not uncommon in Wisdom literature. Whoever is faithful in the smallest things is also likely to be faithful in much, and the converse is also said to be true in regard to dishonesty. Like so many aphorisms and proverbs, these statements are not meant be seen as universal truths but reflect realities that are usually or normally true.[14]

Verse 12 takes matters a step further. It suggests that the real litmus test of trustworthiness is what one does with *someone else's* resources. In an honor and shame culture, where being shamed was worse than being poor, there was a profound concern with reputation: thus we see here that it matters more how one handles other people's property than how one handles one's own. The second half of this saying suggests that even what is one's own is in fact something that is given to a person. This is ambiguous but it probably reflects Jesus's general view that *all* material creation belongs to God, so even what we might count as our own is in fact given to us by God. We are merely stewards of what properly belongs to God.

Verse 13 is famous in biblical studies as a Q aphorism (cf. Matt. 6:24) about being unable to serve two masters, God and mammon.[15] Here money is seen not as a potential resource or litmus test of character, but as a potential master. Interestingly, in Jesus's day sometimes slaves could have more than one owner. In such a case, the service of a slave hurrying from one master's affairs to another's will undoubtedly be less than fully satisfactory to one or the other of the masters.

Thus the saying seems to be "built upon a background assumption that fully adequate service requires an exclusive kind of love and attachment to the master (cf. Exod. 21:5)."[16] More to the point, unless a lord is lord of all he is not really a lord at all. This is the case because the very nature of lordship is all encompassing, at least when one is talking about God. Mammon can't really be a true lord, and if one tries to serve it one can't be a true servant. This is true not least because mammon is only a thing, not a person with whom one can have a servant-lord relationship. It can only be a distorted lordship and a distorted servitude. Some early Jews warned about being "enslaved to lucre,"[17] and Jesus is one such sage. (Notice the teaching about the love of money in 1 Timothy 6:10, which comports with the warnings here.)

Verses 14–15 record the reaction of some Pharisees to this teaching, then Jesus's rejoinder. We are told that some avaricious Pharisees heard all this teaching and literally turned up their noses at Jesus, a gesture of contempt. Luke does not say or suggest that all Pharisees are avaricious, but clearly the teaching of Jesus has pricked the conscience of some who have different views of wealth. It is fair to say that the Jesus movement and the Pharisaic movement were dueling holiness movements, and both of them grounded themselves to a significant extent in wisdom material. These Pharisees perhaps have taken a simplistic approach to some of the teaching in Proverbs and assume that wealth is unambiguously a sign of blessing from God, and so it is not a danger or temptation. Indeed, they may even have assumed that wealth is a reward from God for their righteous behavior.[18]

Jesus clearly has counter-order and counter-intuitive ideas about the matter. He says that these Pharisees are "the ones vindicating yourselves before human beings." And he warns that God knows their hearts, and what humans may commend God may condemn. Avarice or greed is a serious sin in Jesus's view. He is advising his listeners that they should be playing to an audience of One, seeking divine approval of their conduct, not playing to the crowd and assuming that the public's view of money justifies their conduct. The bottom line of Jesus's teaching about wealth and prosperity is that wealth is potentially a great danger to one's spiritual life and well-being. It is a danger because it can so easily cause one to place one's ultimate trust in material resources rather than in God. It's interesting that Jesus doesn't just warn the lost about the dangers of wealth; he warns the saved as well.

Does Jesus then really think that money is inherently evil? No, this would be going too far. Does he think that taxes should be ignored or avoided? This also would be going too far. But it is very clear that Jesus thinks that his disciples should not focus on such things, should not make their life's work about such things, should not place their ultimate trust in such things, and should be prepared to be extravagantly generous to others, especially the poor, if one has possessions. Clearly, believers are to rely on God for even the basic necessities of life. When Jesus urges his disciples to pray about material things, it is never about praying for *wealth*, but always about the basic necessities in life—food, shelter, clothing. Jesus promises that God will provide these basic needs if one seeks the kingdom first, last, and always.

Jesus among the Poor

Now that we have reviewed Jesus's teachings and attitudes about wealth, we can concentrate on what he says about poverty, the opposite of wealth. In this regard, we may also want to ask if Jesus himself was a poor man or a peasant.

It has sometimes been a danger for Christians who are especially impressed with the Sermon on the Mount, particularly in its Lukan form, to romanticize poverty. When poverty is romanticized, it is treated as an inherently good thing, a more spiritual condition than a "middle-class" life, and certainly more spiritual than being wealthy. In the Middle Ages, some monks took "blessed are you poor" to mean that a vow of poverty is some sort of ticket to a more saintly and intensely spiritual life. They pointed to the example of Lazarus in Luke 16, which suggested to them that poverty and even begging—eschewing all of life's material blessings—put one on the inside track to heaven. Is this really what Jesus intended to say about poverty?

We should clear up one misperception at the outset. Sometimes affluent Christians have quoted Jesus's saying "the poor you will have with you always, and you can help them anytime you want" (Mark 14:7 and para.) as if Jesus here lets us off the hook in regard to helping the poor. Even worse, this text has been taken to mean that poverty is an inevitable, intractable condition, and therefore we shouldn't really worry about trying to eliminate it or deal with its root causes. But such interpretations are incorrect.

Jesus is saying that while his listeners will only have him with them for a short while in the flesh, and thus the time to show appreciation for his ministry is limited, there will always be opportunities to help the poor. And Jesus often urged and encouraged helping the poor. In other words, this text is about the rightness of thanking and blessing Jesus while he was on earth, not the lack of necessity to help the poor any time one might have opportunity to do so. Jesus's situation poses a case of priorities and seizing a specific moment—that of his time in the flesh—before it passes.

That misperception aside, let's start the discussion of Jesus and poverty by looking at Jesus's own material situation. Jesus was not a peasant, by which I mean that he was not a landless farmer, a tenant farmer, or a day laborer of any kind. He was an artisan, and an artisan who lived near enough to Sepphoris (a fast-growing city) to have considerable work for a good portion of his adult life in Nazareth. Whether he was mainly a woodworker, a stonemason, or both, he does not appear to have grown up either wealthy or indigent. Nevertheless, the small offering made by his parents for his birth (Luke 2:24; cf. Lev. 12:8) suggests they were rather poor at that early point in the family's life.

To judge from both Luke 4 and Mark 6, Jesus was somewhat educated, for he could read the Torah scroll. This does not mean that he was well-educated or had what we might call higher education, but any degree of literacy would have put Jesus in a minority, associated with persons of higher status in his culture. It is also possible that if Joseph died early, Jesus became the head of his family for a while and was expected as the eldest child to provide for them. But whatever exactly may have been Jesus's material condition when he began his ministry at about thirty years of age, it seems to have changed thereafter.

Jesus forsook both home and family in order to gather up a group of disciples and hit the road. The evidence strongly suggests that Jesus and his disciples, wherever they went, relied on the system of customary Middle Eastern hospitality. Accordingly, Jesus instructs his disciples to depend on invitations into homes when they go out on a mission two by two (Mark 6:8–11). It appears that Jesus and the disciples made Capernaum their base camp, and we know of the house of Peter's mother-in-law in that place. But absolutely nothing suggests that Jesus was ever rich, and there are texts that do indeed suggest that there were times during his ministry when he was very close to indigence. His saying "foxes have holes, birds have nests, but the Son of Man has nowhere to lay his head" (Matt. 8:20; Luke 9:58) indicates just how impoverished he became at one point in his ministry. It appears that Jesus lived by his own teaching, counting on God and the network of social contacts he made by discipling, to provide for the necessities of life, especially when he was on the road.[19] The impression that Jesus did experience poverty at least during part of his life seems to be confirmed in 2 Corinthians 8:9, where Paul says that "for your sakes he became poor."[20]

What of Jesus's stated views on poverty and the poor? Does he warn against poverty in the same way he warns against wealth? Let us consider first the famous beatitude in Luke 6:20 and what follows it in the Lukan form of the Sermon on the Mount. Luke's beatitudes, found in 6:20b–23, take a more personal form than the Matthean ones. Luke writes, "Blessed are *you* poor."[21] This in turn suggests that Jesus sees at least some of his present disciples as being among those who are poor, hungry, mourning, and reviled. These beatitudes are a form of sapiential speech (cf. Prov. 8:34; Pss. 1:1; 2:12; 34:8; 41:1; 84:4; 94:12; 119:2; Sir. 14:1; 25:8, 9; 28:19), but they don't draw conclusions based on what is natural or normal in the human sphere. Jesus's wisdom is by and large a revelatory wisdom, not one deduced from close analysis of nature or human nature. So this beatitude has to do with what Jesus believes will eventually happen to his followers. God will reward or bless them one day.

Makarios (usually translated "blessed [are you if] . . .") has more precisely the sense of "good for you if . . ." or "congratulations if . . ." Jesus is not suggesting in some masochistic fashion that poverty in itself, or hunger in itself, or being persecuted in itself are good things. The sense rather is that faithful discipleship, whatever its difficulties now, will one day be rewarded. The God of reversals will ultimately make things right for his people.

Notice that only the first beatitude speaks of what is true now ("yours *is* the kingdom of God"). The rest speak of future reversals of present deficits or difficulties. Notice in addition that verse 22 associates this sort of misfortune or mistreatment as being caused by the disciples' association with the Son of Man. The disciples may expect the same treatment as their master. The social atmosphere these beatitudes reflect is a situation of considerable opposition to Jesus's ministry, in particular to his teaching and preaching, but also to some of the healings. Verse 23 stresses that the disciples should not be surprised but rather count it an honor to be mistreated for the sake of their message, for the prophets received the same mistreatment from their first hearers. Notice as well the reference to "rewards in heaven." Jesus does not see heaven itself as a reward for faithful discipleship, but like other early Jews he affirms greater and lesser rewards in heaven, based on earthly conduct. Orthopraxy, or right behavior and practice, certainly matters to Jesus.

The parallel woes found in verses 24–26 deal with the precise opposite set of worldly circumstances as those found in the beatitudes. Disciples who are rich, full, laughing, or much praised now may expect a reversal later. The first of the woes makes clear that such disciples already have their reward or consolation, here and now. They may expect hunger or mourning later. The last woe even suggests that praise received now is like the praise heaped on the false prophets of old.

It may be that we are meant to think of beatitudes and woes as interconnected. For example, poverty involves hunger, and hunger can lead to starvation and then premature death, hence mourning. Similarly wealth often involves feasting, laughing, and celebrating now, but if one overdoes those sorts of things there can also be a premature demise later.[22] Obviously neither extreme—extraordinary wealth or desperate poverty—is really a blessing or has a good outcome. It is only the last beatitude and woe that make it explicit that these blessings or woes follow from reactions to Jesus and the kingdom he announces. And since Jesus's disciples are expected to rely on the system of customary hospitality when they journey throughout Galilee and Judea, staying in the homes of those who receive them, it is likely that Jesus is not just offering random social commentary here. He is preparing his followers for the reception they are likely to get when sharing the kingdom and its message with others.

Here I should add that we moderns, imbued so heavily with individualism, often read passages like these as if Jesus is addressing separated, independent, "Lone Ranger" disciples. That is not the case. Consider a passage such as in Mark 10:28–29, where Jesus tells his disciples that there is no one who has left home and family who will not receive brothers, sisters, and houses by the hundredfold. In context he is referring to followers in his own day, and the fact that they can count on each other for hospitality, food, and shelter. More specifically, he is assuring the traveling disciples that they can count on the stationary disciples (such as Mary and Martha, in Bethany) to provide for them when they return home. Jesus's concept of the family of faith is at work here. The point is that disciples have family and homes in many places that they go to, since Jesus's disciples are scattered abroad. Jesus promises even more family and more provisions in the age to come, when the kingdom is fully arrived and consummated on earth.

With attention to this and many other texts, it is clear that Jesus not only cared deeply about the poor and the hungry and the naked (recalling the parable of the sheep and goats in Matthew 25), but that he also acted from time to time to alleviate their plight. He not only heals the sick, but feeds the hungry, and urges tax collectors like Zaccheus to remunerate those from whom they have extorted money. But there is still more.

Jesus even calls his own disciples to sacrificial giving—not merely tithing, but sacrificial giving. That is why we will bring this chapter to a close by examining the familiar story of the widow commended by Jesus for giving to the temple treasury out of her poverty (Mark 12:41–44).

To begin, a comment is in order on Mark 12:38–40, since our evangelist has here set up a deliberate contrast to the widow's sacrificial action. Jesus excoriates scribes (or lawyers) who parade through the marketplace in their "long robes." Worse yet, he says, "They devour widows' houses and for the sake of appearances say long prayers." He probably has in mind scribes/lawyers who have been asked to be guardians of some widow's estate, but have taken more than their fair share of expenses. Then, in order to drum up more lucrative business, they make a show of their piety by offering long prayers in public places. *Jesus has nothing but disdain for the mercenary use of one's faith or piety.* This is made clear here by the use of the technical and damning phrase "to devour a house." The connection between this saying and what follows in 12:41–44 becomes evident. The place where widows would encounter scribes praying is in the temple precincts, the very place that the widow Jesus singles out has gone to make her offering. (The criticism here is likely of aristocratic Sadducean scribes, infamous for their exploitation of the poor and the vulnerable.)[23]

The story begins in verse 41, with Jesus sitting across from the temple treasury and observing people coming forward to make their offerings. There are rich folk who drop much into the treasury, which presumably refers to throwing coins into the trumpet-shaped receptacles found in this portion of the temple. At the same time Jesus sees a poor widow who comes to make her offering, which is all the more impressive since we are talking about a free will offering, not a temple tax. The widow is going above and beyond what is strictly required of her. She gives two lepta,[24] the copper coins of least monetary value that have come to be called widow's mites. There were two lepta in a quadrans, which in turn was worth about one-sixty-fourth of a denarius, the latter being the pay of a day laborer for one day's work. In other words, this widow's gift in actual monetary value is infinitesimally small, especially in comparison to the much greater amounts given by the rich. Jesus then calls the widow to the attention of the disciples, designating her as a model for them. Obviously, it is not the amount of money given but the attitude and action of the self-sacrificial giver that Jesus is extolling here and lifting up for emulation.

This act is especially notable since most widows in Jesus's culture had few means of obtaining money at all. What is more, the widow could have chosen to give only one of her two coins, and so half of her living. The woman is said to have given more *than all the others combined*, for she gave her whole living, however miniscule it might be. She gives out of her poverty and deficit, while the rich give out of their abundance.

There is much to ponder here, but the following points are key. Jesus is commending sacrificial giving to his disciples, not mere tithing (10 percent of income). Jesus does not caution that this woman is being irresponsibly generous. He in fact uses her as a model for his disciples, and what he expects of them is the same sort of lavish generosity and self-sacrifice she exhibits—and which his Father exhibits towards them. God indeed loves a generous giver, but it can be no accident that Jesus characterizes discipleship in general as involving an enormous sacrifice, taking up one's cross to follow Jesus and his example. The widow models self-forgetful behavior, while the scribes criticized in verse 40 display self-centered and self-indulgent behavior.

Moreover, this text indicates that one does not need to be rich to be generous or to have a generous spirit. Jesus does not evaluate sacrifice or generosity on the basis of the amount given any more than he evaluates prosperity or having treasure on the basis of the amount of money made, saved, invested, or the like. His concepts of sacrifice and what constitutes true prosperity, generosity, and well-being differ radically from what many affluent modern Christians seem to suppose.

Some time ago my father was on an every-member canvas team for his local Methodist Church. He was the captain of a team that had as one of its members a young up-and-coming lawyer who wore Brooks Brothers suits and drove a BMW. In an every-member canvas it is the task of the teams to visit members in their homes and gather the pledges for the coming year. One person who was on the lawyer's list was a retired woman living on a fixed income, in a trailer at the edge of town. When the lawyer found the lady, he noted the condition of her tiny yard and the trailer, and was growing reluctant to ask her for a pledge of money. But he went on inside the trailer, where she had fixed him sweet tea and cookies, and they had a grand chat about their church. As the chat wound down, the lawyer rose to leave without asking for the pledge and the widow said, "Wait just a minute, son, I've got my pledge on the fridge." He muttered in return, "That's all right, ma'am, we understand you are just barely getting by. . . ." Before he could finish his sentence she had gotten right up in his face, grabbed him by the lapels, and said, "Don't you take away from me my opportunity to contribute to the ministry of Jesus. Don't you do it, son." Then she handed him her pledge card.

This is the spirit of sacrifice and generosity that Jesus lifted up for emulation in this passage, and it is the very opposite of a spirit of acquisitiveness, of greed, of self-indulgence, of conspicuous consumption. *If there is to be a prosperity gospel worthy of its name, it should be all about the great blessing of giving and living self-sacrificially and how freeing it is to be trusting God day to day for life and all its necessities.*

One more thing. Sacrificial giving is not the same as making oneself an ongoing burden to another person or a group of persons. The widow who gave her liquidatable assets could still go home and be entitled to support from her extended family, for such was the collectivistic nature of that culture. We don't live in a culture like that, in most cases.

In our culture, what may be a sacrifice for one person may well be financial suicide and sudden dependency for another. It's not a solution to poverty to fill up one hole by digging another one somewhere else. When we look at Paul's teaching in Galatians 6, we will see that burden bearing and burden sharing are *both* encouraged in the body of Christ.

Each modern Christian individual will have a different set of life circumstances and responsibilities to consider when evaluating what amounts to sacrifice on his or her part. It can't be quantified across the board by simply waving a 10 percent flag, or some other formula.

Here it may help us to remember the story of the pig and the chicken. When the farmer demands eggs for breakfast, the chicken complains that she must make a great sacrifice. To this lament, the pig only snorts, "Sacrifice, you are just making a free will offering! When the farmer demands bacon, then there is a sacrifice involved." Sacrifices look different for different persons; they involve different percentages of giving according to one's life circumstances.

The point is that since we all must live by faith, trusting God, and as disciples we are all called to sacrificial living ("take up your cross daily") *and* sacrificial giving, it is important that we keep short accounts with God in regard to our resources, erring on the side of generosity and giving (without making ourselves a nuisance or ongoing burden to others). God loves a generous giver.

And the interesting thing about letting go of possessions and giving is that it probably benefits the giver as much as the receiver. Giving frees us from being possessed by our possessions and forces us to continue to trust God on a daily basis. Giving is a way of relinquishing direct personal control of one's life, giving it back to God as a living and ongoing sacrifice. It is an act of faith, a sign that one is prepared to trust God and leave the outcome in God's hands.

5

James's Rich Wisdom

Can anybody remember when the times were not hard and
money not scarce?

—Ralph Waldo Emerson

Despite the fact that James was not a follower of Jesus during his
ministry (John 7:5), it is clear that after Easter he was profoundly
indebted to his brother and his brother's teachings for his viewpoints
on a host of subjects. These certainly included money, wealth, and
poverty. Like his brother, James approaches ethical discussions from
a sapiential or wisdom point of view. And like Jesus he draws heavily
on the tradition of counter-order wisdom. Because the Letter of James
may well be the very first Christian sermon that treats the subject of
wealth and poverty at some length, we will take time to unpack two
of the most significant passages from its text, one from James 2 and
the other from James 5. Initially James may not have been enamored
with Jesus's teaching, but this sermon shows that over time he became deeply influenced by his brother's teaching in the Sermon on
the Mount and elsewhere.

James 2: Impartiality in a Stratified Society

James 1 introduces the topics James will discuss in his homily.[1] What
we are dealing with in James 2:1–5:6, then, is supporting arguments

79

for the theses already alluded to or enunciated in the first chapter. James presupposes a Jewish Christian audience, so in his sermon he uses Jewish themes, ideas, stories, wisdom sayings, analogies, and Scriptures.

Chapter 2 consists of two major sections (vv. 1–13 and vv. 14–26). The first section deals with the matter of showing partiality, especially to the rich over the poor. In the background is the idea that God is no respecter of persons, with the implication that his people should not be either. Here our author is picking up and continuing earlier discussions found in sapiential literature that warn against favoritism arguments that stress God's impartiality.[2] James addresses his audience as "my brothers," so we may be sure that he considers them Christians. However, they are Christians under construction and, from James's point of view, they require instruction.

James begins this section by stating that the issue at hand is showing favoritism or partiality, and what he intends to prove is that partiality and faith in the glorious Lord Jesus are incompatible. That some Christians purport to exhibit both together is unacceptable and reprehensible because it amounts to a violation of God's command to love.

A further important point about this crucial thesis statement is that the key phrase reads literally "keep/hold the faith of the Lord." Though this is regularly rendered "faith *in* the Lord," this is not exactly what James says. If that was what he meant he could have used the prepositional phrase beginning with the Greek word *en*. This in turn may well suggest that Jesus is seen as the exemplar of impartiality, and believers are to keep the "faith of the Lord" (i.e., his trustworthy and faithful ways) by modeling themselves on his behavior. In a stratified world of "showing" or "giving face" to one person or another who was thought to be of higher status (and accordingly more honorable), Jesus and James both deconstructed this practice of sucking up to the well-heeled.

It is significant that the phrase we find here ("with your acts of favoritism") includes a term that literally means "to receive face." The same term is found in Leviticus 19:15 in the Greek translation of the Old Testament (known as the Septuagint), which reads: "You shall not render an unjust judgment; you shall not receive/give face to the poor or defer to the great: with justice you shall judge your neighbor."[3] This suggests that one must be impartial to *all* persons, not showing favoritism to either the rich or the poor. The phrase refers to the kind of persons who make judgments on the basis of "face," that is, the outward appearance of someone, just as we might speak about the face value of something. The point that James is making here cannot be overemphasized. He is not suggesting that one should show partiality to or "preferential option for the poor." He is saying that we should not show favoritism to the rich, which is unfair to the poor; nor should we slight the poor and so dishonor them. All persons should be treated fairly, regardless of their socioeconomic status. Of course one can argue that since there is imbalance in a fallen world full of self-centered acquisitive persons, God is concerned about balancing the scales, about justice for all, and in a fallen world this may appear to be partiality for the poor. I think this is what James has in mind, and it is in accord with what Leviticus says about impartiality.

In verse 2 James proposes a hypothetical example of showing partiality. We know that the example is probably hypothetical because James uses a conditional clause beginning with "if" plus a subjunctive verb, which suggest that he views the example as a more probable future condition. His example is a definite possibility, one that is to be avoided, but not necessarily something that is already plaguing the audience. Here we have proof from an example, with the punch line coming in verse 4 and proving the point that partiality to any persons and faith or faithfulness to the example of Christ are inconsistent. Those who really follow Jesus will not be partial judges of other persons, and certainly not of other Christians.

So what sort of gathering or audience is James addressing in these verses? Is it a Jewish synagogue, the Christian church, or some sort of Christian law court? Even though the Greek word *synagōgēn* is used, it seems unlikely that James is speaking in a Jewish synagogue. James implies that his Christian audience has some control over what is happening when visitors enter their meeting. And he refers to the gathering as "your assembly," which surely implies a Christian rather than a strictly Jewish setting. The word *synagogue* is used elsewhere in early Christian literature to refer to the church (see Heb. 10:25).[4]

Nor is it likely that James is speaking of some sort of Christian court of law. Not only does he use a different word for *law court* in this passage (*kritēria*, v. 6), but also there is evidence that visitors are present (1 Cor. 14:23), along with well-to-do people who have become members of the Christian community, including the Jewish Christian community in Jerusalem (see Acts 4:34–5:11, for example). Nor is 1 Corinthians 6:1–6 an entirely apt parallel since Paul *says* they are going to pagan law courts, but argues for them to settle differences and conflicts among themselves in the community. This implies that there wasn't a Christian court of law already established when Paul was writing in the 50s. The fact that James says "*your* synagogue" rules out a reference to pagan courts here. It is also probably a mistake to read later Jewish law court traditions back into this text.

Rather, James is probably speaking about and to a Christian worship assembly. If it was like Jewish worship assemblies during that time, held in a small building or home, some might have to stand while others could sit down. It is evident from later sources that visitors were allowed in and ushered to a specific spot, a duty deacons were later assigned. It was Jewish custom to have special and honored places in the synagogue for special people and benefactors (cf. Matt. 23:6; Mark 12:30; Luke 11:43, 20, 46). It would not be at all surprising if Jewish Christians carried this custom over into their meetings. Both the poor and the wealthy examples here are likely viewed as visitors since both are directed where to sit. Nothing is said about why the rich or poor man came into the assembly, and the issue of partiality is raised not in regard to the behavior of either one but rather to the behavior of the person seating them, that is, the Christian usher.

James finds the usher's behavior unacceptable. The contrast between the rich and poor man may be played up a bit, but the wearing of gold rings and fine clothes was widely practiced among well-to-do Jews and Gentiles in first-century culture, and the description of the poor man as being dressed in worn clothing and being dirty may suggest that he is a beggar.[5] It's possible that the reference to a man with a gold ring indicates a person of high rank, perhaps a potential benefactor to the congregation.[6]

Verse 3 is quite clear that the Christian usher who is seating these visitors is judging them purely on the basis of appearances—which often leads to partiality: "The rich person is invited to sit rather than to stand, to proximity rather than to distance, to comfort or prestige rather than to discomfort and dishonor."[7] The Greek verb here can have the sense of "to look upon with favor" as is clearly the case in Luke 1:48 and 9:38, the other two instances of this term in the New Testament.[8] Notice as well that the verb is plural, suggesting that this sort of favoritism involved more than one Christian usher or leader. Verse 3b has the phrase "sit at my feet," which is sometimes a technical phrase for "be my disciple," but that is not likely meant here (cf. Luke 10).

In verse 4 various commentators take the phrase "among yourselves" as evidence that the visitors are Christians. This is not a necessary inference, however, because—as I have already stated—the focus is on the usher. The problem is that these Christians are welcoming visitors but they're showing partiality, which is unacceptable regardless of the visitor's social status, faith, or their wealth and honor are concerned. When the visitors are with the believers they are to be considered part of the worshiping community. The partiality is happening in Christian worship, which is the last place it should happen since worship is supposed to be where God is perfectly glorified and people are treated as God treats them.

Judging by appearances (v. 3a) is judging by a false and all too fallible standard (v. 4). It is probably right to hear echoes of the teaching of Jesus here, from parables like those found in Luke 14:7–14 and 16:19–31. In those parables we see the dynamics of the dramatic contrast of rich and poor, and how each is treated in this life.

In verse 5 James begins another argument. We have a statement about the poor, followed by two about the rich. Three rhetorical questions are asked, all of which expect the affirmative answer "yes" from the audience. The function of such rhetorical questions is to force the audience to answer the questions for themselves, but in a way that coheres with the conclusion James wants them to draw. Partiality to the rich is bad for the poor and makes no sense because the rich are oppressors of Christians. The three questions serve as a way of amplifying the point that partiality is inconsistent with Christian faith. The most disturbing question is left for last, as a climax. James suggests that a highly ironic situation has arisen—those to whom God expects us to be most compassionate are being oppressed, and those who most blaspheme God's name are being flattered and privileged.

The idea of God showing special concern for the poor is, of course, well known in the Old Testament (cf. Deut. 16:3; 26:7). Jesus also, in Luke 6:20, picks up the idea of the election of the poor, and we find similar thoughts in Paul (1 Cor. 1:27ff.—God chose the lowly things of this earth . . .). James 2:5 speaks of the poor who are poor from the world's point of view, but rich in what really matters (faith) and what comes through faith (the inheritance of the kingdom). Though James does not romanticize poverty, he is referring to the economically poor, not merely those who are "poor in spirit" (Matt. 5:5). In fact he will suggest that spiritually these folks are far from poor.[9]

It is thus a wrong line of interpretation to suggest that poverty here has simply become a religious or spiritual concept. The social dimensions of poverty must not be overlooked, even if James does share some ideas about the pious poor. The poverty spoken of is both physical and spiritual, as is the wealth, but no one person in the contrasting example embodies both kinds of wealth or poverty. The poor in question are believers who may be rich in faith, but this does not give permission for other, wealthier Christians to treat their physical poverty as if it does not matter. Elsa Tamez puts it this way: "I do not mean that the poor are not pious, but only that if we make the poor and the pious synonymous then real economic oppression and God's concern for this very class of people are lost. The rich become the pious poor and the poor rich in piety, and the economic order and the unjust power stay as they are. Thus the rich always come out ahead; they are rich in real life and piously poor before God and thus heirs of God's reign."[10]

Equally true are the remarks of Alfred Plummer, who states that James "does not say or imply that the poor man is promised salvation on account of his poverty, or that his poverty is in any way meritorious. . . . He is spared the peril of trusting in riches, which is so terrible a snare to the wealthy. He has greater opportunities of the virtues which make man Christlike, and fewer occasions of falling into those sins which separate him most fatally from Christ. *But opportunities are not virtues, and poverty is not salvation.*"[11] Notice as well that the poor here are said to be heirs of the kingdom. This is the only reference to the kingdom in James, and it seems to be used in the sense of something that one inherits or enters into in the future, not the present (probably echoing Jesus's beatitude on this matter; see Matt. 5:3).

Verse 6 refers to disrespect shown to those upon whom God has especially showered favor. Paul shares a similar view about shaming those who have nothing; the social context, which presupposes disunity and favoritism in the assembly, is also similar (see 1 Cor. 11:22). This is a very unwise course of action, and verse 12 indicates that the perpetrators are accountable for such actions on judgment day. The standard of judgment is the law of liberty, that is, the new law of Christ that combines something old and something new.

Finally, playing up to the rich also doesn't make sense. Generally speaking, at that time it was the rich who oppressed believers and hauled them into court. James may have had a particular incident in mind, but the remarks seem to be generalizations. Thus, we have irony here. The church is oppressing one poor fellow who came to visit its worship, while the rich oppress "you," that is, the church as a collective whole. In effect, James asks: What sense, then, does your behavior make considering God's word and standards? In verse 7, the rich are labeled blasphemers—blaspheming Jesus's good name, perhaps because they profess to be pious but their deeds are impious.

In verse 14 James broadens the previous discussion to the more expansive topic of faith and works. Here James asks his Christian audience whether or not a faith without works is useful. His grammar indicates that the question is not likely just a hypothetical one. The second remark also takes the form of a question: "Is your faith able to save you?" This is a rhetorical question to which the answer implied is no—if by faith one means the type of (faulty) faith that James is attacking. Crucial to understanding this verse is recognizing the significance of the definite article in the Greek before the word *faith*. The question should be translated, "Can that (sort of) faith save him?" Notice also that the discussion here has now moved from talking about visitors to addressing the assembly of the faithful, the brothers and sisters in Christ. At this juncture James clearly focuses on the Christian treatment of fellow Christians.

There follows (in vv. 15–16) a little parable, also begun with the word "if," thus indicating a condition that is future but probable. Certainly there were plenty of destitute Christians in the first century, in need of aid from the community. James portrays a scantily clad and hungry brother or sister. The Greek word *gymnoi* need not imply nakedness, but rather under- or poorly clothed. This person is so indigent that he or she doesn't even have enough food for today. The glib verbal response in verse 16 (along the lines of "hope you are well fed and clothed") is meant to seem shaky and shallow. It sounds pleasant enough, even concerned in a superficial way. But in fact this is an anti-Christian and unloving response that James considers unacceptable. Beneath the surface is the idea that actual deeds of mercy are, for those who profess and have real faith, not an option but an obligation.

"Go in peace" is literally what the person says to the indigent brother or sister. The saying could mean "have no anxiety," but in fact what we have here is a stereotyped parting formula. Although it could have the fuller sense of "blessings" (cf. Gen. 15:15; Exod. 4:18; Judg. 16:6; 1 Sam. 20:42; Mark 5:34; Luke 7:50), it often meant no more than "goodbye." That is what seems likely here. It appears also that we should translate the Greek verbs in verse 16 as middles, not passives, in which case the saying means "warm yourself" and "feed yourself," not even "be warmed" or "be filled" as a sort of wish. If this is right then the person in question (i.e., the brothers or sisters being addressed here) is being very callous indeed. That person is juxtaposing warm words with cold deeds and, like so many others since, is saying in effect "Pull yourself up by your bootstraps" or "Do it yourself." Quite clearly, what is being requested by the beggar is not some luxury item, but the necessities of life, clothing and daily bread. But even these are not given. As Luke Timothy Johnson says, the problem "is not the form of the statement [depart in peace], but its functioning as a religious cover for the failure to act."[12]

To this behavior James rejoins, "If you say you have faith and fail to help—of what use is it? What good does it do you or anyone else?" Possibly, in verse 17, we should translate *kai* as "even," reading the sentence as "so *even* faith, if it does not have works, is dead by itself." James has thus made two key points: living faith necessarily entails good deeds; and faith and works are so integrally related that faith uncoupled from works is useless or dead. Peter Davids summarizes the text well:

> For James, then, there is no such thing as a true and living faith which does not produce works, for the only true faith is a "faith working through love" (Gal. 5:6). Works are not an "added extra" any more than breath is an "added extra" to a living body. The so-called faith which fails to produce works (the works to be produced are charity, not the "works of the law" such as circumcision against which Paul inveighs) is simply not "saving faith."[13]

If we think that James has been stern thus far on the matter of wealth and the rich, we will soon discover he has just been warming up his polemics in James 2. In James 5, to which we now turn, the author becomes even more polemical and strident.

James 5: The Rich Are Heading for Hell

In order to feel the full force of James's sermonic rhetoric, I offer here a fresh translation of the first six verses of James 5:

Come now, you rich, weep, howling at the wretchedness that is coming upon you. Your wealth has rotted and your cloak is moth-eaten, your gold and silver is covered with rust and its poison will be (for) evidence against you [or a testimony against you] and it will consume your flesh like fire. You hoarded (it) in the last days! Behold the wages of the worker who mowed your fields (estate) which have been withheld by you cries aloud, and the cries of those who reaped have come into the ears of the Lord Almighty. You lived in luxury upon the earth and you were pleasure-loving [self-indulgent]. You have fattened yourselves [literally, "your hearts"] in the day of (your) slaughter! You condemned, you murdered the righteous (one)! Does he not actively resist you (now)?

James 5:1–6 deals with a somewhat different group of people from the merchants referred to in 4:13–17, though we may note the similar opening address at 4:13 and 5:1—"Come now." This could suggest that 5:1–6 is dealing with a subset of those who are referred to in the previous paragraph; those (including merchants) who have actually managed to become rich. The problem is that it appears that James may not even be dealing with Christians of any sort in this paragraph, nor with the same sort of entrepreneurs and businesspersons he has mentioned previously.

James 5:1–6 apparently refers to the wealthy landed class, those who own fields or possibly estates. J. B. Mayor notes: "The terms chosen have reference to the different kinds of wealth, *sesēpe* to corn and other products of the earth, *sētobrōta* to rich fabrics, *katiōtai* to metals; giving examples of corruption arising from an external cause (the moth), or internal, whether deep-seated rottenness or superficial rust."[14] These rich people are apparently sedentary, not traveling businesspersons, and they are known for their agricultural estates, rich clothes, and accumulation of goods and silver coins. James stresses that such people are already on the way to judgment at the end of time, and certainly shouldn't now be admired, emulated, or served. Furthermore, there is a key rhetorical signal that we are not dealing with the same group of people in 4:13–17 and 5:1–6. The style of the former text is the diatribe while the latter is more like an oracle of woe. What this suggests, rhetorically, is that the former group are those whom James thinks he has and can still have a dialogue with, while the latter are beyond any persuasion.

From a rhetorical standpoint, an orator knew quite well that what one said near or at the end of a discourse would be what was left ringing in the audience's ears. Since James's document was meant to be preached out loud to congregations, there were probably few among his hearers who would be able to read and peruse this material later, treating it as a text. This in turn puts a premium on the final argumentation in a discourse, and the peroration that follows it. The fact that James has been addressing the issue of the rich and riches at several points throughout the discourse, and now returns to it in a major and polemical way, suggests that this is perhaps the most important concern he has for the Jewish Christians he is addressing. The temptation of Christian merchants and others to become clients of the landed wealthy, or even to attempt to emulate them, must have been considerable. Commentators have understandably had a hard time seeing how James 5:1–6 comports with the more gentle tone of 4:13–17, but the answer is really not that difficult. James is speaking about a different group of people here, the non-Christian rich who in some cases seem to have been oppressing some of those in his (Christian) audience. Whether these rich people are pagans or Jews, James has saved his most stinging critique for here, the very end of the discourse.

Verse 1 begins in a rousing fashion, with James summoning the rich to view in advance their coming demise. The form of this beginning is not unlike what we find in Hosea 5:1 and Amos 4:1 or 5:1, where we have prophetic oracles of woe (cf. Matthew 23; Revelation 18). So those who are knowledgeable in James's audience will know that they are about to be in for some heavy rhetorical weather. In essence, the rich are invited to view their funeral in advance. They should begin to weep and wail because of the miseries that are heading right their way. Isaiah 13:6 speaks of wailing because the Day of the Lord is near, and this is certainly what James has in view.

Verses 2–3 expand on the plight of the rich. Note the perfect tense of the verbs that are used here: "has rotted," "has become mildewed," "has rusted." The rot and rust and ruin have already set in, destroying their assets—and they don't even know it! The judgment is so certain that one can say it has in effect already begun. Everything that the rich put store in has only stored up wrath and fire for them. The phrase "will eat your flesh like fire" probably draws on the analogy of the rust—just as the rust will eat away and destroy their coins, so the fire of judgment will eat the flesh of the rich![15] While gold and silver do not literally rust, they do pit, tarnish, and require polish, which is likely what James has in mind. (We may also note that sometimes coins were made with impure silver or gold, and these coins were subject to corrosion.) Notice as well that James talks about the money standing as "evidence against you" in the last days. Luke 12:23 may well be in the background here: perhaps James was reflecting on Jesus's parable about the rich man and Lazarus when he penned this salvo.

Verse 3b is significant: "You have laid up treasure in the last days." If one reads this to mean "you have stored up wealth in the last days," which it certainly can mean, then James is accusing them of hoarding in the age of judgment that which specifically has absolutely no means of security in that age. They may think they are laying funds aside for their golden years, their own last days, but in fact they are hoarding things that will end up testifying against them in *the* last days.[16] We know the teaching of James's brother about laying up treasures in heaven, which is contrasted with laying up treasures on earth where moth and rust do destroy (see Matt. 6:19–20). But James takes the image a step further. As one scholar puts it, "Here he condemns the rich for 'living in the last days' . . . but nevertheless living as if they had all the time in the world and their judgment was not near."[17]

And So?

When one reads through this sermon carefully, paying attention to the details, it is hard to imagine it ever being preached today in America or any other wealthy country, even by non-prosperity preachers who don't have any affluent people in their congregations. Showing partiality, sucking up to the wealthy, if not glorifying the success of the wealthy, ignoring the warnings in Scripture about the dangers of wealth and how it can deaden one's soul and prevent one's real dependence on God, and even put one on the path to everlasting destruction—all are part and parcel of modern church life in our affluent world. And even worse is the glorification of the rich and of affluence through prosperity preaching, the very opposite of James's message.

Having said all of that, we should remember that James does not glorify poverty. His concern is with equity and impartiality across the board (a clear concern of Paul's as well, as we shall see). James believes strongly that Christians who are better off have an absolute obligation to help those who are less fortunate, including especially the less fortunate Christians with whom they have routine contact. If they just say "feed yourselves" or "cloth yourselves," they are parade examples of how so-called faith without good works is as dead as a doornail. It will not save anyone.

We might ask here whether James was somehow exceptional in his views on wealth and poverty. One way to test whether or not he was merely an extreme preacher is to examine what is said about such matters in other parts of Scripture, such as the book of Acts. So, at this juncture we turn to Luke's two-volume work, Luke-Acts, and consider the issues of wealth, money, and poverty in that context. We will discover that when it comes to warnings about the dangers associated with wealth and money, James is neither extreme nor exceptional.

6

Wealth and Poverty in Luke-Acts

> Business, you know, may bring money, but friendship hardly
> ever does.
>
> —Jane Austen

We have already had occasion to notice that there is considerable material in Luke's Gospel about wealth and poverty, money and prosperity, and the like. Here we will take some time to discern in more detail what Luke's views are on these matters. Scholars have long noted that Luke has a particular interest in wealth and poverty, so his writings demand close scrutiny. Though Luke has more to say about wealth and poverty than the other Gospel writers, he actually has less to say about money per se.

Wealth and Poverty in the Gospel of Luke

The Greek word *ptōchos* occurs with considerable regularity in the New Testament. Its literal meaning is "beggar," though it is often used more broadly to refer to the poor in general. It is by far the most common term in the New Testament for the destitute (occurring thirty-four times). This term basically refers to persons who lack the basic necessities of life (food, drink, clothing, shelter, and land, as well as freedom and honor). While it is true that the term *poor* can be used metaphorically in a spiritual or theological sense, the vast majority of usages in the New Testament refer to literal, material poverty. Some texts could be debated (for example, "our Lord Jesus, though he was rich, became poor, so that you through his poverty mighty become rich" [2 Cor. 8:9]), but none of the debatable texts occur in Luke-Acts.

One of the major problems in the treatment of texts about poverty and wealth in the New Testament is anachronism, that is, reading modern economic situations back into the first-century Roman world. For example, modern readers examining New Testament texts on poverty often fail to see the problem as systemic, preferring to think it is caused by individual laziness or lack of initiative. While it is undeniable that sometimes laziness is *a* cause of poverty (notice the criticism of the sluggard in Proverbs), there are much larger, more systemic factors and forces at play in Jesus's world. These include: famine and crop failure; slavery; the intricate web of patron-client relationships that made it almost impossible to get ahead in life unless one were well connected; the oppression of being under foreign rule, either directly or indirectly, and the enormous tax burden and theft of land that entailed; and the highly patriarchal character of society, especially in the Holy Land, which limited women's roles and often prevented them from accumulating possessions or wealth. When we add to this picture basic human greed and other forces and effects at work in a fallen world, we can see why it is not at all adequate to speak in late Western individualistic terms about poverty and wealth in the Bible.

Perhaps nowhere in the New Testament is there a clearer attempt to connect the macrocosm of general society with the microcosm that was the Jesus movement, both before and after Easter, than in Luke-Acts. Luke sees things from a wider and more historically conscious perspective than the other evangelists. And though his theme is salvation history, he understands God's divine intervention to mean trouble for the high and mighty, while it is good news for the poor. In other words, Luke refuses to spiritualize what salvation really entails for the least, the last, and the lost, as well as for the most, the first, and the found.

Luke, more than any other New Testament writer, uses salvation language in both senses the term had in the Greco-Roman world, where salvation could mean literal healing or rescue from some danger as well as redemption in a theological sense.[1] And here we note that while theological salvation and physical health in the literal sense often go together in Luke-Acts (a person is healed or rescued as well as saved in the more spiritual sense), salvation and *wealth* typically do not. Indeed, for Luke persons of higher social status who are saved are more likely to be depicted as divesting themselves of wealth, at least in part (see, for example, the story of Zaccheus). While Luke does not reject the system of patronage as it existed in his world, he does believe that Christians who are patrons must do what they can to alleviate poverty, particularly the poverty of their fellow believers. With this preamble, let's turn directly to some key texts in Luke's Gospel.

I have already suggested that we need to note Luke's heavy stress on the economic aspect of the gospel and salvation. We see this throughout his Gospel, beginning with Mary's paean of praise exulting that God "has brought down rulers from their thrones and lifted up the humble. *He has filled the hungry with good things, but has sent the rich away empty*" (Luke 1:52–53). We also see it in the teaching of John the Baptist. When asked by the "brood of vipers" what they might do to manifest repentance and so avoid the coming judgment, John says, "The person with two tunics should share with the one who has none, and the one who has food should do the same." Tax collectors also come to be baptized. "Teacher," they ask, "what should we do?" John tells them, "Don't collect any more than you are required to collect." Then some soldiers ask, "And what should we do?" John replies, "Don't extort money and don't accuse people falsely—be content with your pay" (Luke 3:10–14). We also find Luke contrasting blessings on the poor with woes on the rich: "But woe to you who are rich, for you have already received your comfort. Woe to you who are well fed now, for you will go hungry" (Luke 6:24–25).

It becomes apparent that in Luke's view the coming of the kingdom in Jesus has brought an economic reversal of fortunes. It is also striking that in the Lukan version of the Sermon on the Mount we find these words: "And if you lend to those from whom you expect repayment, what credit is that to you? Even 'sinners' lend to 'sinners' expecting to be repaid in full. But love your enemies, do good to them, and lend to them without expecting to get anything back. Then your reward will be great . . ." (Luke 6:34–36). In Luke, the challenging command to love one's enemies is fleshed out to mean "lend them money if they need it, and don't expect it back." This is especially striking because in Jesus's society there were no assumed obligations to be generous to one's opponents.

There is more. In Jesus's woes on the Pharisees we hear, "But give what is inside the dish [or what you have] to the poor, and everything will be clean for you" (Luke 11:41). In Luke's later use of Sermon on the Mount material (Luke 12:33) we encounter his counsel to the rich young ruler: "Sell your possessions and give to the poor. Provide purses for yourselves that will not wear out, a treasure in heaven that will not be exhausted, where no thief comes near and no moth destroys."

Later Luke brings this saying to life in Acts 6, where we have both Barnabas, who is obedient and honest in his generosity, and Ananias and Sapphira, who are deceptive in their giving. So we see that for Luke, Jesus's specific teaching to the rich young ruler is broadened and applied to Jesus's followers in general. Accordingly, we must assume that Luke did not think that Jesus's advice to the rich young ruler was a special or exceptional case. This is made emphatically clear in Luke 14:33: "In the same way, those of you who do not give up everything you have cannot be my disciples." This presumably is part of what Luke has in mind when he intensifies the saying of Jesus about the cross so that it reads, "those who would follow me must deny themselves and take up their cross *daily*, and follow me" (Luke 9:23).

When Jesus is dining at a Pharisee's house he deliberately tries to deconstruct the usual customs of hospitality and social networks in his world by telling the host, "When you give a luncheon or dinner, do not invite your friends, brothers, sisters, relatives, or your rich neighbors; if you do they may invite you back and so you will be re-paid. But when you give a banquet, invite the poor, the crippled, the lame, the blind, and you will be blessed. Although they cannot repay you, you will be repaid at the resurrection of the righteous" (Luke 14:12–14). In various texts, then, Luke's Jesus stresses giving with no thought of return, so as not to involve one's self in the customary social networks of reciprocity.

Such examples could be multiplied, but these are enough to show that there is a definite emphasis in Luke's Gospel on showing how commitment to Christ affects what one does with one's possessions. But is there a larger theological vision that binds such individual sayings together? As it turns out there is, and to get at that vision in Luke's Gospel we need to deal with several texts in depth. We will begin with the programmatic sermon of Jesus in Luke 4.

The sermon at Nazareth is set up in 4:14–15 by stressing that Jesus returned to his home region in the power of the Spirit, then traveled through Galilee preaching in various synagogues to much acclaim ("everyone was praising him"). Luke 4:16–30 presents a crucial turning point in the story. Up to now there has been no opposition to Jesus. He has received only acclaim, even as early as his visit to the temple when he was twelve. But when Jesus later in the Gospel goes home to Nazareth, something surprising happens.

Luke has carefully structured this material so that the narrative that follows this sermon will demonstrate how the Scripture he cites here (Isa. 61:1–2) is fulfilled.[2] We can see this from the following:

Luke 4:18–19	Luke 4:38–44	Luke 8:1–3
vs.18—Preach Good News		vs.1—Preach Good News
Recovery of sight to the blind	vs. 38—Jesus heals Simon's mother-in-law	vs. 2—Healing evil spirits and illnesses in women
	vs. 40—Jesus heals sick	
Set at liberty the oppressed	Demons cast out	Examples of exorcism—Mary
vs.19—Proclaim acceptable year of The Lord	vs.43—preach Good News to other cities	Compare 8.4–15

If we compare Luke's account of this story to its parallels in Mark 6:1–6 and Matthew 13:53–58, it seems clear that Luke has intentionally placed this story at this juncture in his presentation even though the event itself likely happened later in the ministry of Jesus. The reason for this is plain—this story provides a preview of coming attractions, making clear not only the character of Jesus's ministry and mission and the fact that it entails the fulfillment of Scripture, but also the nature of the response he will receive. While many will be impressed with Jesus, this does not mean most will be persuaded to follow him. Faith in Jesus will involve much more than being impressed by his teachings or deeds.

Luke 4:16 makes clear that Jesus continued to be an observant Jew, for we are told that, as was his custom, he was in the synagogue on the Sabbath. Note the comment here that Nazareth is where Jesus was brought up, rather than where he was born. This verse also indicates that Jesus was literate, something that could only be said of about 10 percent of those who lived in Jesus's day and world. It also shows that Jesus can read Hebrew, which is unusual since early Jews in Galilee spoke Aramaic rather than Hebrew. Notice too that Jesus does not choose the scroll from which he will read; he is simply handed the Isaiah scroll. Jesus must search out and find the text he wishes to read from Isaiah. There were no chapter and verse markings in first-century scrolls; indeed there was seldom much separation between words or sentences in them. It therefore took some looking and knowledge of where to look to locate a particular text. In addition to suggesting his education, this also says something about Jesus's piety. He is familiar enough with the Scriptures to know where particular passages are found.

The text Jesus reads is Isaiah 61:1–2, but there is also an allusion to Isaiah 58:6. Perhaps Jesus was teaching during the exposition time of the service, where it was appropriate to comment on more than one text, since at this point in a traditional service readings from both the Law and the Prophets would have already taken place.[3]

The normal synagogue procedure in Galilee would have been to read the selected text in Hebrew and then translate or paraphrase it into Aramaic, which is presumably what Jesus did. Luke, however, does not know the Semitic languages and so he simply follows the Septuagint, the Greek translation common in his time. The text incorporated from Isaiah 58:6 is the phrase "to send the oppressed away in liberty."

But there are also significant omissions from the Isaiah text: one, omitted from Isaiah 61:1 is the phrase "to heal the brokenhearted," which seems an odd omission in light of the character of Jesus's ministry of compassion. And two, omitted from Isaiah 61:2 is the phrase "and a day of vengeance," which is a more understandable deletion. The citation of this Scripture has prompted an enormous amount of discussion, especially as it relates to liberation theology.

What is sometimes lost in such discussions is that Luke 4:19 alludes to the year of Jubilee, the so-called year of God's favor that occurred once every fifty years, or once in a lifetime for most people. This was the year when persons would be released from debts of various sorts, slaves would be freed, the land would lie fallow (be given a Sabbath rest), and persons would return home to their original family property (Lev. 25:10–13). That Jesus proclaims such a year is now inaugurated is crucial, especially in light of what Hillel had earlier suggested about debts being extended beyond the Jubilee year, so the poor could obtain loans.[4]

Even more intriguing is the fact that AD 26–27 *was* a Jubilee year, so one wonders if this is in fact the year that Jesus began his ministry.[5] In any case the use of this text, if applied by Jesus to his ministry, indicates clearly that there was to be both a spiritual and a social dimension to Jesus's work. Release of captives from demonic possession, debt, and sin would all be part of Jesus's ministry. Likewise, concern for both those who were economically poor and the poor of spirit would be a hallmark of his ministry. So too would healing miracles, including healing of the physically and the spiritually blind. This means that both traditional and liberation theologians are correct in some of what they have concluded about Jesus and his ministry, based in part on this text. Traditional theologians are right to note that by citing this text Jesus is indicating that he was anointed by the Spirit quite specifically for preaching, including evangelizing the poor. And liberation theologians are correct in the observation that in addition to preaching there is also the matter of sending the captives away free, which involves more than just proclamation.

Verse 21 is probably not meant to indicate the entire content of Jesus's message, which should be translated "and he began to tell them 'this Scripture has been fulfilled in your ears.'" Jesus, then, is reading this text in light of the customs and laws associated with the Jubilee year and with an awareness that his ministry has inaugurated the end times. This would have surprised his first listeners. They would have readily assented to the notion that God would fulfill his promises, but the idea that they are fulfilled on this day, in this synagogue, in the presence of this audience, is another matter.

Verse 22 seems to suggest that the audience is favorably impressed with what Jesus says, for it says that they all bore witness to him and "marveled" at his gracious words. But the marveling must be set next to the querying that soon followed: "Isn't this fellow Joseph's son?" The Lukan answer to this question is both yes and no. Yes, legally Jesus is Joseph's son; but, no, he is not an actual physical descendant of Joseph's bloodline. Notice that Luke, like Matthew's parallel (13:55) but unlike Mark (6:3), comments on Jesus's relationship to Joseph. There is then some intended irony in the question here. The real question seems to be: "Who does this son of an artisan think he is—a prophet?"

Verse 23 provides Jesus's retort. It includes not only the proverb "Physician, heal yourself," but also a challenge: "What we have heard happened in Capernaum, do also here in your native place." The issue here is that Jesus has performed no wonders or miracles in his hometown that might make his audience receptive to the notion that he is a fulfiller of Scripture, a prophet of the end times, or the like. It needs to be kept in mind that the northern prophetic tradition focused on Elijah, who was in the first place a miracle worker as well as a giver of oracles.[6] It is thus understandable that the hometown crowd might expect Jesus to perform miracles if he wanted them to believe in the dramatic claims about his ministry and himself. But as verse 24 suggests, Jesus thinks he is laboring against the hometown curse, against unbelief: no prophet is accepted in his native place.

What follows in verses 25–30 is for the most part unique to the Lukan account of these proceedings. The thrust of the polemical teaching here is that Jesus is comparing his own audience to previous generations of hard-hearted Israelites who were not receptive to the ministries of Elijah or Elisha, so that foreigners benefited from their ministries in a way that many Israelites did not. The examples of the widow of Zarephath and Naaman the Syrian are cited (cf. 1 Kings 17–18; 2 Kings 5). As one scholar puts it, "The point . . . [is] that unbelief has created a situation where possibilities are not realized and benefits do not flow, a situation parallel to the occasions when the prophetic ministry of Elijah and that of Elisha (prophets raised up in Israel and for Israel) brought no blessing to Israel."[7]

This scene also has a close parallel in Acts in the story of Stephen (compare Acts 7:52 to Luke 4:24), another text where the crowd responds to the accusation of rejecting the prophets with anger and even violence. The parallel is even closer than it might appear at first glance, because verse 29 probably suggests that the audience is following the procedure for stoning—the offender is taken outside the city, pushed off a hill or cliff, and then stoned. Yet Jesus in some unspecified manner slips through the angry crowd and goes on his way (compare Luke 22:3, 5 to John 7:30; 8:59; 10:31, 39).

For our purposes the importance of this sermon can hardly be overestimated. Jesus believes that he is bringing in the kingdom of God and inaugurating the Jubilee year, and this should lead to a profound change of the social order. Things can no longer be business as usual. It is the Jubilee message of release from debts that Jesus is including in his salvation program for Israel. And when that is coupled with the theme of reversal, what we are meant to think is that Jesus's ministry gives a preview of the ultimate or end-time conditions: there will be no more hunger, nakedness, homelessness, famine, violence, or poverty.

Jesus's action and those he requires of his disciples are meant to provide a foreshadowing and a foretaste of the final Jubilee in the consummated kingdom. Part of the gospel is then calling even tax collectors (as well as others) to debt relief, to generosity, to eliminating poverty, to giving up the lifestyles of the rich and famous and instead spending that time and money on compassionate ministries. Furthermore, Jesus is depicted as believing that there are eternal consequences to whether or not one heeds this good news for the poor.

In the parable of the rich man and Lazarus this sort of thinking is made even clearer. This parable, found only in Luke 16:19–31, may well reflect the fact that Jesus draws on elements of a familiar story, but then makes the story his own in order to make his own points.

The Egyptian story of Setme and his son Si-Osiris was likely extant before the time of Jesus. That narrative recounts the story of an Egyptian who was allowed to return from the dead to deal with an Ethiopian magician who was besting Egypt's best magicians. Before Si-Osiris returns to the land of the dead, he and his father observe two funerals—one of a rich man and one of a poor man, the former buried in sumptuous fashion and the latter buried without ceremony. Setme declares that he would rather have the lot of the rich man, but his son corrects him and says that he would do better to wish for the fate of the poor man. In order to justify this view he takes his father on a tour of the seven halls of the otherworld. The rich man is shown being tormented, while the pauper is elevated to a high rank. The son then explains to the father the fate of those whose bad deeds outweigh their good ones, such as the rich man, and the fate of those whose good deeds outweigh their bad ones, such as the pauper. There were also at least seven Jewish versions of this same story, all of them focused on the reversal of fortunes of the rich man and the poor man in the afterlife. Jesus of course will tell this fictional story in his own more Jewish way.

Luke 16:19 begins by painting a clear picture of a rich man who is self-indulgent, wearing royal purple robes and fine linen and feasting sumptuously every day. He lives like a king (see Prov. 31:22). In fact, it is not impossible that Jesus is alluding here to King Herod Antipas, who, like the rich man in Jesus's story (v. 28), had five brothers.

The contrast with Lazarus described in verse 20 is stark and dramatic. Lazarus is a poor man with body sores. He lies at the gate of the rich man's house. In other words, he is readily visible to the rich man as he comes and goes from his home on a daily basis. But the rich man does nothing to help him. While the poor man longs even for the scraps and leftovers from the rich man's feast, he is given nothing. Even the scavenging dogs, who may have gotten some scraps, come and lick the poor man's sores, adding injury to insult. Not surprisingly, the poor man soon dies. He is carried by angels to Abraham's bosom, presumably in the highest level of heaven, in Paradise.[8] The image conveys the notion that he is right beside Abraham, and is now his bosom buddy so to speak, his intimate. Notice that it is not stated that the poor man even received a proper burial.

It is, however, stated in verse 22 that the rich man dies and is (properly) buried. Verse 23 adds that the man is in Hades and is being tormented. He looks up and sees Abraham far away, with Lazarus "in his bosom." Thus in verse 24 the rich man calls upon Father Abraham (which makes clear the rich man is a Jew) and asks him to send Lazarus to him with "cool" fingers (dipped in water) to touch his tongue, which is on fire as he agonizes, engulfed in flames. In other words, the rich man, even in Hades, thinks he can still treat the poor man like a servant, or someone beneath him on the social ladder.

In verse 25 Abraham breaks it to the rich man gently (calling him "child," since he himself has been addressed as father) that he received good things during his earthly life. Lazarus in his earthly life received evil things, "but now" conditions are reversed. The poor man is comforted and the rich man is in agony without relief. Verse 26 makes very clear that there can be no reversal of the reversal once one dies and is in the afterlife. There is no shuttle service from Hades to Abraham's place, only a great chasm fixed by God between the two otherworldly destinations.

Accepting that his own fate is sealed, the rich man then lobbies Abraham to send Lazarus back from the dead to his father's house to warn his five brothers, so they will not end up in Hades as he has (vv. 27–28). But Abraham refuses this request as well, saying that they have Moses and the prophets and that should be enough: they should listen to them.

This parable suggests many things, not the least of which is that behavior in this life has eternal consequences. It may also suggest that Jesus believed, as did some other Jews, that eternal punishment and reward begin immediately after death. However, since this is a parable, that idea should not be pressed too far because elsewhere Jesus talks about resurrection and final judgment on the earth when the Son of Man returns. More importantly, in this entire chapter the focus is on the problems associated with wealth and the truth that it is hard for a rich man to enter the kingdom of God. Jesus's sympathies are clearly with the pious poor. In his cultural setting, Jesus is viewed as critiquing the Pharisees' older sapiential assumption that wealth is simply a blessing from God. But his wisdom has passed through the crucible of reflection on the last days, and so he expects a reversal of the injustices experienced in this life. Wealth and poverty are not reliable guides to how God evaluates a person.

Perhaps the reversal theme also explains another reversal of early Jewish expectations in such a parable: the rich man is nameless but the poor man is named. In this we glimpse the idea that, while Jews are viewed as God's chosen people, individual Jews do not make it into Paradise simply because they are elect. Their course of life and behavior, including the way they treat the poor, affects their eternal outcome. Some of these same themes will be reiterated and expanded in Luke's second volume.

Wealth and Poverty in Acts

There has been a tendency in scholarly work on Acts to conclude that Luke has gilded the lily a bit, meaning that he presents more of an ideal rather than a real portrait of early church life, of his hero Paul, of the inevitable triumph of the gospel, and so on. The problem with this analysis is that Luke repeatedly admits that there are serious problems in early Christianity, throughout the period he covers (roughly AD 30–62). That said, it is difficult to discern which things Luke is telling us are normal or characteristic of early Christianity and which things are a rule or standard that Christians should aspire to, particularly in matters of practice. But if one of the criteria for seeing something as normative from Luke's perspective is finding a repeated pattern, then it will serve us well to look closely at what is said in Acts 2 and 4 about the characteristics of the Jerusalem household meetings. Here property, wealth, and sharing things in common figure prominently in the text.

In Acts 2:42–47 the disciples are said to devote themselves to four things: the teaching of the apostles; *koinōnia*, or sharing in common; the breaking of bread; and prayer. The text goes on to suggest (vv. 43–47) that the disciples do not in any full or decisive way separate themselves from their Jewish context and heritage. For our purposes verse 44 is most crucial. We are told that this earliest cadre of disciples shares all things in common. Verse 45 more fully explains this by adding that they sold their possessions and real estate, then distributed the proceeds *to any who had need* within the community. The verb here is in the imperfect tense, indicating that this was not a one-time activity but rather an ongoing one. In other words, we are not to see this activity as simply reflecting an initial burst of enthusiasm after the first Easter. It is a recurring practice that continues whenever the need arises.[9]

It needs to be noted that here Luke is not talking about some sort of mandatory confiscation and redistribution of goods and property, with everything then parceled out equally to every member of the community. This becomes very clear from a close reading of the Ananias and Sapphira story, in which Peter reminds them that even after they liquidated their assets it was still their choice as to how and to what degree they would dispose of the proceeds or give them away. The point here is that no one was claiming any exclusive right to property, and there were concerted efforts to make sure that no Christian was in want. Christians take care of their own. They do not, for example, rely on the charitable acts of the temple apparatus or a synagogue, or some general dole for the poor in Jerusalem. They take matters into their own hands. Thus what we see here is the family of faith concept put into practice.[10]

Acts 4:32–37 in fact serves as an introduction to what we find in the beginning of Acts 5, and so an introduction to both a good example of Christian generosity and self-sacrifice in Barnabas, and a bad example of deceit in the case of Ananias and Sapphira. In short, these two specific cases show how money and property should and should not be handled and dispensed by Christians who have such resources. In association with these two early passages in Acts, we should note that in the Greco-Roman world friendship involved sharing in common goods and property. In other words, there was reciprocity between social equals. But here Luke is not talking about a reciprocity cycle among equals. Instead he is talking about *giving without thought of return, giving to those less fortunate—to those who are not one's social equals.* Put a bit differently, Luke's admonition should not be seen as simply an expression of Greco-Roman friendship conventions, but rather the kind of self-sacrifice that would take place within a family context. At the same time, Luke has no problem with the idea that there will be economic inequities for various reasons. Thus he encourages patronage, setting forth good and bad examples of it. In this regard Barnabas stands out as the good exemplar.[11]

Acts 4:32 is the crucial verse here: "no one called personal or private anything that belonged to him. Everything was shared in common."

Notice that this practice is tied to being "of one heart and mind." This behavior is not merely a formally endorsed practice, it is a practice that reflects the heart desire and agreement within the community about the way things ought to be. There ought not to be any Christian in need or want. This is a point that Luke reiterates and emphasizes. Clearly, no one is claiming owner's rights, exhibiting selfishness or possessiveness. I suggest that this grew out of what we spoke of in the first main chapter of this study—a realization that the earth is the Lord's and the fullness thereof, and therefore all things belong to God. In turn, we are simply God's stewards and should ask the proper question: what would God have me do with this property that he has blessed me with or gifted to me?

Acts 4:34–35 explains how the early church dealt with needy Christians. What Luke means here is not that there were no needs or needy persons, but that when this situation was recognized it was soon remedied. One suspects that this is a social practice the earliest Christians were keen on because of the earlier teaching of Jesus himself, including his identification with the disadvantaged and the poor (Matt. 25:35–40). The Old Testament was equally emphatic about the matter: "There will, however, be no one in need among you because the Lord is sure to bless you in the land" (Deut. 15:4). What is also described here is the liquidation of assets such as land or houses, turning them into money. Nothing is said here about the transfer of ownership of property from disciples to the apostles as, for instance, followers transferred property to their leaders in the contemporary community at Qumran. Nor is there any evidence of the control or ownership of all property by the community. As we have noted, Peter's remarks to Ananias and Sapphira rule that out.

Notice as well that Luke calls those who give the property here "owners," and as Peter makes clear with Ananias and Saphhira, the giving and the amount given were voluntary. It ought to be done, but the decision to do it is in the hands of the individual in question. There is no compulsion from the community or the apostles: Freely you have received, freely give, seems to have been the principle. And thus we conclude that what is described here is that Christians who have higher status are selling some of their property and giving the proceeds to the apostles for distribution. It would not be accurate, however, to call this some sort of early communism. It was more a form of communitarianism, where the sense of community is so strong, and the sense of obligation to one's brothers and sisters in

Christ so clear, that such actions are seen as natural, necessary, normal, and not forced or compelled. It is a consummation devoutly to be wished that we had more Christian communities like this today. Finally, this leads to the conclusion that the problem with Ananias and Sapphira is not that they keep some of their liquidated assets but that they lie to the church and the Spirit about what they have given and what they have kept, no doubt to improve their honor rating in the community.

As we analyze Acts 4–5 closely and then turn to Acts 6 and the issue of the widows who were in need of support, what seems to be implied by all this is that funds were given on an ad hoc basis when a need was recognized and made known. That is, there was not, at least initially and as depicted in chapters 2–5, a weekly or regular collection for the poor in the community, or a regular periodic distribution. But Acts 6:1 reflects a time later than that suggested in Acts 2–5, a time when there were both Aramaic- and Greek-speaking widows in the community. Apparently by that time there had developed a regular or daily distribution of food for the widows, and only the Greek-speaking ones were being neglected. This seems to have been a problem created in part by the continued growth of the community, hence the need to assign the Seven to the task of making certain that there was no one in need in the community. Notice that in Acts 6 we are dealing with the more specific issue of widows, and not need in general in the community. Taking care of widows was one of the major Jewish concerns addressed in the Old Testament, in a world where widows could own little or nothing and so were rarely able to support or take care of themselves.

A profitable study could be done of all the passages about the vulnerabilities and care of widows in the Bible, and it would show that the obligation to widows was carried over from the Israelite practices into early Judaism and then into early Christianity, especially perhaps in its earliest phase when the Jewish-Christian ethos was dominant (compare Exod. 22:22; Deut. 10:18; 14:29; Ps. 146:9). Widows in this Jewish patriarchal culture were in most cases entitled to maintenance but not inheritance. This made them especially vulnerable and so it is not a surprise that Jesus on various occasions comments on their plight.[12] But they are just a special part of a larger problem. Jerusalem was constantly plagued with drought and famine, which led to periodic and chronic food shortages. At a time when people had little or no personal reserves and lived day to day (praying for *daily bread*), the need for repeated and regular care of those who are less well-off was ongoing.

Later we will have occasion to talk about Paul's collection for the poor Jewish Christians who were living in Jerusalem, but note here that the collection in the Pauline churches was not just a collection for the widows, but for the whole Jerusalem church in the 50s, which also was struggling after several periods of drought, famine, and food shortage. Paul was working at a time when the Jerusalem church had largely been cut off from the synagogue and temple; thus there was no local organization that could help in times of need, making their situation especially urgent. It is no surprise that Paul, who had grown up in Jerusalem, made it his personal mission to remember the poor in that city. The collection he took up was mostly from Gentile churches, with hopes that this generous gesture would help bind those churches to the Jerusalem church.

And So?

In his helpful study on faith and wealth, Justo González draws the following conclusions about Luke's presentation of wealth and poverty, particularly in Acts:

> No matter how much Luke's Gospel has made of renunciation, what is described in Acts is a community where people relinquish their possessions, not for the sake of renunciation, but for the sake of those in need. . . . The goal is not an abstract or dogmatic notion of unity nor a principle of purity and renunciation but meeting the needs of others.
>   It is inevitable in such a community that those who are most generous, such as Barnabas, will arouse the jealousy of others such as Ananias and Sapphira. Yet the very fact that the book of Acts tells the story of both Barnabas' generosity and the deception of Ananias and Sapphira immediately after describing the community of goods indicates that this is neither an attempt to paint the early community in idyllic tones, nor to describe a dogmatically communistic commune. Peter clearly tells Ananias (Acts 5:4) that he was under no obligation to sell his property, and that having sold it he did not have to bring the proceeds to the community. Thus Acts describes an imperfect community with its share of liars and jealousy. . . . The self-understanding of this group . . . is such that "no one said that the things which he possessed was his own." Yet the actual working out of the sharing that this implied

depended both on the needs of those who had no possessions and on
the free will to share on the part of the more fortunate.[13]

This is certainly a fair and balanced assessment of what we find in
the first seven chapters of Acts, and it means that in fact Luke does
not here see himself as presenting an unrealizable and unrealistic ideal
of Christian community when it comes to the matter of wealth and
poverty. In other words, Luke views this as a viable guideline for his
own community, his own time. Were he here today, presumably he
would say the same about our Christian communities.

We have covered a lot of ground briefly, but what we have uncov-
ered is that Luke is insistent that the church attend to the problems
of the poor and needy in the community of Jesus's followers, not
leaving them to rely on the system of standing hospitality in early
Judaism in the Holy Land. He does not see this as a mere option but
as an obligation for the followers of Jesus, especially if they want to
emulate his own practices. After all, had he not fed the hungry five
thousand? Had he not raised the widow of Nain's son so she would
have a means of support (Luke 7)?

Luke seeks to paint a portrait of the earliest Christian community
that shows that the church, as a sign of the unity of open and sincere
hearts, has addressed the needs of its members. The basic principle is
that *no follower of Christ should be in need or want.* Luke presents
his argument in favor of this view by repeatedly revealing how the
early church dealt with the matter. Along the way he also makes clear
that he is not advocating for some central storehouse of goods or a
centralized equal distribution of all property to all the community
members.

Luke is content to point out the obligation of patrons to do something about the situation, but even then he stresses through the voice
of Peter that what and how much they give is a matter for the giver
to determine. Giving needs to be done with integrity and not for the
achievement of honor within the community, as seems to have been
the unfortunate case with Ananias and Sapphira. Equally important,
Luke stresses that the giving should be done without thought of return, which is to say that giving must be done without the intent to
produce a response that sets in motion a reciprocity cycle.

As we turn to the Pauline letters, we will find more of this sort of
approach, as well as other issues related to wealth and poverty that
Paul must address.

7

Paul—On Work, Remuneration, and the Love of Money

The rule is not to talk about money with people who have much more or much less than you.

—Katherine Whitehorn

There is, especially in some forms of low-church Protestantism, a notion that Paul advocated a principle of ministers earning their own living and raising their own support for ministry. Sometimes this approach is even called tent-making ministry, based on what Paul says about supporting himself by making or mending tents in 1 Corinthians 9 and Acts 20. Unfortunately, this approach misunderstands almost everything Paul says on the subject of a "workman being worthy of his hire." It fails to interpret Paul's letters in light of the actual social world and social practices that Paul experienced. In fact, as we shall see, Paul is quite happy to receive support, as long as it doesn't involve the entangling alliances of patronage. And so in this, as in many other things, the problematic situation in Corinth, and Paul's response to it, should not be taken as indicative of a general principle in regard to ministers raising their own support. Indeed, what 1 Corinthians itself suggests is that the congregation had an obligation to give and provide support, but Paul had the freedom to reject that payment and support himself, if he so chose. While the subject of money and the church has always been sensitive business, this was and is even more the case when one is dealing with the issue of ministers and their remuneration.

Bearable Burdens and the Burden of Proof

Perhaps the best place to begin a full discussion of Paul's view of money, possessions, and remuneration is with what is probably his earliest letter, Galatians (probably written in AD 49). Sometime in the decade of the 40s, after promising the Jerusalem church on one of his visits that he would "remember the poor," Paul embarked on a series of strenuous missionary journeys to plant churches in various places in what we now call Cyprus and Turkey. The Letter to the Galatians, written from Antioch shortly after some of those travels, discusses a variety of matters of church conduct. Our focus will be on Galatians 6:1–10, the climax of Paul's letter.

The structure of Paul's final argument in Galatians is reasonably clear. It falls into two sections, 6:1–5 and 6:6–10. The first section focuses mainly on the law of Christ, the latter on the aphorism that one reaps whatever one sows. Within these two sections there appears to be an alternation between words about corporate responsibilities to one another and words concerning individual accountability.

> 6:1a—corporate responsibility to correct a sinning Christian
>
> 6:1b—individual accountability—look to yourself (you singular)
>
> 6:2—corporate responsibility to bear the burdens of one another
>
> 6:3–5—individual accountability—test your own works, bear your own load
>
> 6:6—corporate responsibility to support those who teach
>
> 6:7–8—individual accountability—what one sows will be what one reaps
>
> 6:9–10—corporate responsibility—everyone should do good to all, especially to fellow Christians.[1]

Throughout this argument Paul seeks to make clear what the Christian life should look like.

A central question for interpreting all of this advice is: How specific is this advice, really? Is Paul simply collecting and arranging some general maxims here that he sees as reasonably apt for his converts' situation, or is this advice more pointed and particular? Without neglecting the spiritual dimension of this text, I suggest that Paul's argument has a social dimension usually overlooked by modern commentators. But this was not always the case. John Chrysostom, in commenting on this material, not only sees 6:6 as an explicit reference to the financial support of Christian teachers, but sees verses 7–10 as an expansion of the same idea of giving material aid to others, especially those in the household of faith.

At first glance, it may appear that this passage about bearing one another's burdens counsels spiritual and personal support. But in a detailed and convincing study, J. G. Strelan argues that the primary subject of this entire passage is matters financial.[2] In support of this conclusion he notes that if Greek cultural and linguistic contexts are taken into account, the following comes to light. First, the word *prolambanein* ("anticipate" or "do beforehand") in 6:1 can refer to money received previously, in advance, or given as a retainer, and the word *paraptōma* ("wrongdoing") can refer to an error in the amount of payments. In 6:2 we find the word *baros* ("weight"), which is used at least half the time in Paul's letters to refer to financial burdens. We also find the word *bastazein* ("take up," "bear"), which can mean to carry, as in assuming someone else's indebtedness, and the word *anaplēroun* ("replace," "fulfill"), which often means to pay in full, fulfill a contract, or make up a debt. In 6:4 appears the word *dokimazein* ("prove by testing"), which refers regularly to the testing of the genuineness of metals and coins (cf. Prov. 8:10; 17:3), and the word *ergon* ("work"), which is often used in reference to trade or commerce (cf. Rev. 18:17). In Galatians 6:5 the word *phortion* ("burden," "load") regularly refers to freight, cargo, wares, or merchandise. In 6:6 the word *koinōnein* ("contribute") can refer to sharing a financial burden or holding material resources in common (cf. Acts 2:42ff.; 4:32), while *logos* ("word") can refer to an account (of expenses) (see Phil. 4:14–15). In 6:7–8 we have the language of sowing and reaping, and in the only other places where Paul uses this language, the context indicates that money matters are at issue (cf. 1 Cor. 9:10–11; 2 Cor. 9:6). In 6:9–10 the term *kairos* ("time") can refer to the time when a payment is due. Finally, we note the argument of John Bligh that the "household of faith" in 6:10 refers to the Jerusalem Christians,[3] to which Larry Hurtado has added the suggestion that 6:10 is about the collection for the Jerusalem church.[4]

We must bear in mind that Paul is quite capable of using the language of material things in a spiritual sense, as when he uses the various terms and ideas associated with slavery to speak of salvation and service in the Christian community. But, taken as a whole, the argument that 6:1–10 focuses on finances is persuasive. This means that, far from offering merely general maxims here, Paul in his concluding argument provides us with some very specific examples of what it means to bear burdens and follow the law of Christ. Galatians 6:1 begins this subsection with a concern about some sort of law that Paul believes his converts are accountable to, and in some danger of violating in the future. There are two options. Either Paul is speaking of a transgression against a secular law code or against a code he will mention in this very context, namely the law of Christ. The parallels between Galatians 6:1 and the teaching of Jesus in Matthew 18:15 lend credibility to the latter suggestion: "If your brother sins [against you], go and point out the fault when the two of you are alone. If the brother listens to you, you have regained that one."

In both Matthew 18:15 and Galatians 6:1, then, we hear about what to do when a follower of Christ is found to be sinning. In both texts the concern is for the restoration of the wayward believer, not disciplinary treatment of him or her. What we will discover is that Paul in his final argument begins each section of his argument (vv. 1 and 6) with his own restatement of two of the sayings of Jesus. These must be considered part of what Paul means by the law of Christ.

There has been considerable debate about what Paul means by "you, the spiritual ones" in 6:1. Is he referring to a particular, elite group of Christians in Galatia? This is unlikely on two counts. First, whenever we have had the address "you" previously in this letter, it has always referred to all of Paul's Gentile converts in Galatia who are the recipients of this letter. Second, Paul throughout Galatians has spoken of all Christians as having the Spirit (3:2–5, 14; 4:6, 29; 5:5, 16–18, 22–23, 25; 6:8). He has also emphasized that the Galatians received the Spirit when they were converted: indeed, this is what distinguished them or set them apart as Christians (see 3:1–5). However, there seems to be a contrast between the "transgressor" and the "spiritual ones" in that the spiritual ones are all those in the Galatian assemblies who are not involved in the transgression or sinful matter. In essence, then, Paul is warning the spiritual ones that they must "watch out, lest any one of you [singular] be tempted." Paul is reminding the disciplinarians that they too are morally vulnerable and must take care not to get caught up in the same transgression. There is no room for any attitude of moral superiority.

Galatians 6:2 should probably not be viewed as connected to 6:1, since there are no connecting particles here. Notice that the word *one another* is in the emphatic position, stressing putting others first. The words *ta barē* refer to some sort of burden or load; it was not uncommon for the phrase to indicate a financial burden.[5] As noted above, about half the time in the Pauline corpus the term and its cognates refer to a financial burden (as in 1 Thess. 2:5–9; 2 Thess. 3:8; and 2 Cor. 12:16). That meaning is quite possible here as well. Remember the exhortation in the Jesus tradition to "give to everyone who begs from you, and do not refuse anyone who wants to borrow from you" (Matt. 5:42), to which we might add the probable allusions to the Jesus tradition in James 2:15–16 (on helping the needy in deed and not merely in word).

A strong case has been made by Richard Hays that Paul has in mind here the example of Christ as the ultimate burden-bearer. And even if we limit our considerations to what Paul says about Christ in Galatians, we hear of "Christ who gave himself for our sins, so he might deliver us out of this present evil age" (1:3–4). We also hear in 2:20 about "the Son of God who loved me and gave himself for me," and in 3:13–14 about Christ who "redeemed us out of the curse of the law by becoming a curse for us" (probably alluding to the notion of a burden-bearing scapegoat). To this we may add the phrase "the faithfulness of Jesus Christ," a shorthand way of speaking about Christ's obedience even unto death on the cross, in conformity with God's plan that he bear the burden of the punishment for human sin.

Furthermore, we must take into account the language in Galatians about both Paul and other Christians bearing the image of Christ, even the image of his passion. Paul understands his own life as a recapitulation of the life pattern shown by Christ. The most important text here is 2:19b–20: "I have been crucified with Christ. No longer do I live but Christ lives in me."[6] In other words, this pattern of burden-bearing and self-giving is seen as the essence of what Christ was about, so also at the heart of what Paul means when he speaks of the law (or main principle) of Christ.

Galatians 6:3 may not begin a new subject, but rather may be a further development of what has just been said. Here Paul is chastising those who think they are something, but in fact are nothing. This could be a chastisement of those who think they are too good or important for burden-bearing. This stands in stark contrast to the pattern of Christ, who, while he was certainly something and somebody special, emptied himself and made himself as nothing, taking on the form of the servant (Philippians 2). Paul is probably here making an only slightly veiled reference to those who are not following the pattern of Christ in the way they live and behave, those who are basing their estimate of self on the basis of false criteria. The word *phrenapata* refers to deception, in this case self-deception, and presumably the conceit involved leads a person to be unwilling to bear other people's burdens, or perhaps unwilling to shoulder the burden of the shame of the cross (see Gal. 6:14–15).

It is important to keep in mind how easy boasting and self-promotion were in an ancient honor and shame culture, and at the same time how counter-intuitive it was to suggest that someone of higher status should actually step down and become a servant of those who are less well-off or more burdened. The pattern of Christ and the message of the cross went against many of the major social assumptions in Greco-Roman culture. Few pagans were eager to take on the jobs of a slave, which, of course, included various forms of burden-bearing.

Verse 4 shows that Paul is indeed mindful of contemporary conventions about when and what sort of boasting or self-praise is appropriate or inappropriate.[7] Notice that he does not say that all boasting is inappropriate but that one may consider one's own work a cause for pride, not that of a neighbor's. Notice also that Paul here is not talking about the final testing of one's works by God's judgment, but rather of critical self-appraisal.

So what is Paul referring to when he says in verse 5 that each person must carry his or her own load? Does this not contradict what he has just said in verse 2? Is there some reason why Paul uses a different word for *burden* here than in verse 2 regarding bearing one another's burdens? It is not likely that Paul would flatly contradict himself within the span of three or four sentences. One could argue that here Paul is saying that persons who can be self-supporting should not expect others to take care of them, but at the same time if one is able to help bear the burdens of someone else who really needs the help, he or she should do so. In other words, the two verses are about the difference between an egocentric imposition on other people's goodwill (v. 5) on one hand, and the Christian duty, self-sacrificial in character, to help each other with life's burdens (v. 2) on the other.

It is possible, however, that Paul intend to give a slightly different nuance to the word *burden* here than in 6:2. The term here seems to have been used less frequently in a metaphorical or nonmaterial sense. For instance, the word *phortion* in other Greek literature commonly refers to a soldier's pack.[8] It is definitely unlikely that Paul is promoting the Greek philosophical notion of self-sufficiency here in verse 5. Paul doesn't believe in that idea: he believes in the sufficiency of dependence on God. Nearer to the mark about this verse is the comment by James Dunn that the "mature spiritual community . . . is the one which is able to distinguish those loads which individuals must bear for themselves, and those burdens where help is needed."[9]

If we are meant to see a connection between verses 5 and 6, with the latter qualifying the former, then another view is possible. I suggest the following hypothesis: (1) the relationship between the words *work* (*ergon*) and *burden* in verses 4–5 must be considered. Paul is talking about a person's work or gainful employment and how one assesses it; (2) the burden in verse 5 is indeed a financial one—each person should carry his or her own financial weight if at all possible and not be an unnecessary burden on another's patronage or charity; (3) the *exception* to this rule is the one offered in verse 6 that alludes to the teaching of Jesus when he says "a worker is worthy of his hire," a saying that Paul draws on in several places to affirm that he, and other evangelists and missionaries, had the right to financial support from the congregations they served. Even if these proclaimers could refuse such aid if they wished, they had a right to it so that they could be freed up to concentrate on sharing the gospel; (4) "all good things" in verse 6 refers to material support for the teacher given by the teacher's disciples; (5) the agitators and whoever followed their lead in insisting on circumcision, however, were mocking God, sowing unto the flesh, and were going to reap the whirlwind in due course; (6) the warning is given to the Galatians lest they follow in the footsteps of the agitators; (7) the Galatians should not grow weary of doing good of the sort specified in verses 1–2 and 6 as there will in due course be reward for such; and (8) this meritorious doing should concentrate on the household of God, but should include all people within its scope. If I am right about the above there is more of a flow of thought to the argument, especially its second part, than is usually supposed. In all events, we again see that Paul does not contradict himself with "bear one another's burdens" in verse 2 and "all must carry their own loads" in verse 5.

The second half of Paul's argument in Galatians 6:1–10, like the first half, focuses primarily on financial matters. As with the first half of the argument, Paul begins with his own paraphrasing of a teaching of Jesus, which he now applies to his Galatian converts' situation: "But the one being taught the word should share all good things in common with the one teaching." This exhortation is based on Jesus's saying found in Luke 10:7, which Paul expounds on at some length in 1 Corinthians 9:3–14. In that text we also have the discussion about Christians being scrutinized or examined by others (9:3), a discussion about the right to be supported as teachers of the word (9:6, 13–14),[10] and the statements about teachers sowing spiritual good and reaping material benefits (9:11). These parallels must be allowed to have their full weight, and they make it likely that throughout Galatians 6:6–10, Paul is talking about pertinent financial (and spiritual) matters. It is, however, difficult to know whether or not Paul here is making a veiled reference to himself, and the Galatians' obligation to support him. This is certainly a topic that comes up regularly in Paul's letters (see 2 Cor. 11:7–11; 1 Thess. 2:9; 2 Thess. 3:7–10; Rom. 15:24; Phil. 1:5; 4:15). Then too, the phrase "the good things" appears elsewhere in the New Testament with reference to material support, aid, or food (Luke 1:53; 12:18–19).

Is the singular reference to "the one teaching" to be taken literally? If so, then a reference to Paul may be meant. The alternative, however—and perhaps the more likely reading—is to suggest that Paul has in mind some local Christian teacher or teachers in Galatia who are deemed worthy of the Galatians' support. Then the reference to "good things" may well prepare us for the concluding exhortation in verse 10, in which case the "good" there alludes back to the "all good things" here, including material and financial aid.

Paul quotes, in verse 7b, what was likely a proverbial saying found in both Greek and Jewish literature[11] in order to provide backing or a basis for the warning just given. For our purposes, what is important to stress is that in the only other places where Paul draws on this metaphor (1 Cor. 9:10–11 and 2 Cor. 9:6) financial matters are the issue. This sort of use probably echoes the discussion in Proverbs 22:7–9: "The rich man lords it over the poor, the borrower is the lender's slave. He who sows injustice reaps disaster and the rod of anger falls on him." Notice also that the exhortation not to grow weary in doing good also shows up in 2 Thessalonians 3:13, at the end of an exhortation about earning one's own living and resisting idleness.

If we put all this together, the meaning of verses 7–8 becomes clear. Verse 7b is a statement about anyone, including Christians, which Paul then applies in verse 8 using his flesh-Spirit antithesis. I suggest that the sowing unto the Spirit that Paul has in mind is the supporting of proper teachers, materially and otherwise. Verses 6–8 must be read as a whole. In verse 8, then, Paul contrasts an essentially self-directed act, getting oneself circumcised, with concern for and actions on behalf of others. The former is of the flesh, while the latter is of the Spirit. This comports with the overall theme of this section, stressing other-regarding actions and warning against selfish ones. (It also comports with the same sort of discussion of the relationship of present deeds and future destiny in Rom. 2.)

Verse 9 warns against weariness in doing good, and promises that at the appropriate time in the future a harvest will be reaped by doers of good, if they do not give up. Since this verse is grammatically connected to verse 8 we should probably see a qualification here of the remark about sowing and reaping in verse 8. This verse like the last suggests that the payoff is in the future. And there is a condition placed on reaping. It will not happen for individuals, even for Christian individuals, automatically. They must not grow weary of and give up on well-doing. Here as elsewhere Paul admits the possibility that those currently in Christ might commit apostasy, or give up the faith, and so miss out on eternal life and the rest of the benefits that come with the consummation of the kingdom (see 5:3–4). Paul is not saying that a person is saved *by* good works, but that where there is time and opportunity for doing such things, one will not be saved without them. They are not optional extras in the Christian life.

In verse 10 Paul concludes his argument by making a little clearer what he means by sowing unto the Spirit, a little clearer what verse 9 was meant to imply. The introductory phrase "Therefore then" here, as elsewhere in Paul, signals the conclusion or the main point of an argument (see Rom. 5:18; 7:3; 25; 8:12; 9:16, 18; 14:12, 19; Eph. 2:19; 1 Thess. 5:6; 2 Thess. 2:15). Its presence here makes quite clear that it is inadequate to see this section as simply individual maxims with little or no connection to one another or with the larger argument of the entire letter. The qualifier for what follows is "as time allows" or "as we have time [and opportunity]." Paul says that we Christians (both himself and his audience here, as in verse 9) should "work the good to all." Paul has absolutely nothing against working or good works. His earlier critique had to do with very a specific sort of work—the works of the law. Indeed, Paul throughout this whole argument in verses 1–10 argues for the necessity of good works by his converts, as well as the necessity of avoiding bad ones. Doing good to all would at the very least include charitable works towards the needy and the poor. Paul qualifies his final exhortation by urging that efforts should especially be made on behalf of the household of faith.

Paul thus concludes this argument (and the Letter to the Galatians) with some practical exhortations about what they ought and ought not to be doing. Far from receiving vague and general maxims, the Galatians are told specifically that they are to restore erring Christians, bear one another's burdens, support their teachers financially, and do good to all, especially Christians. In all of this they will be following the pattern of life and teaching of Jesus, which Paul calls the law of Christ.

The principles we find here enunciated in Paul's earliest letter will play out in more detail in his subsequent letters. These principles include the following. First, Christians should provide for themselves and carry their own financial burdens, and those who will not work should not be expecting to eat, freeloading on the congregation or the congregational meals.[12] Second, when there is a need the congregational members are expected to step in and bear one another's burdens; this is a very specific fulfillment of a commandment of Christ to his disciples. And third, teachers are worthy of financial support and congregations should expect to support them, though a teacher can refuse such support for a variety of reasons. This leads us quite naturally into discussing what Paul says about the remuneration of ministers in 2 Thessalonians 3 and 1 Corinthians 9.

Remuneration of Ministers: A Working Hypothesis

Anachronism, a potential pitfall when reading and studying the Bible that we noted earlier in this book, can especially be a problem in reading Paul's letters. The mistaken assumption is that conditions today are identical to those in Paul's day, so that we do not need to understand the social differences between then and now to understand correctly the words of Paul. This sort of thinking, when it comes to the issue of money and remuneration of ministers, is particularly flawed because it fails to take into account the ancient system of patrons and clients, and the problems that accrued when one became enmeshed in the web of duties to a patron. Paul, above all things, needed to remain free wherever he went, to pursue ministry on his own terms without entangling alliances. If support could be garnered and given without strings attached, well and good. If it could not, then Paul would fend for himself. Paul carefully circumvents the encumbrances of a reciprocity and patronage culture while trying to offer the gospel of God's free grace. It was tricky business, and there were places where people did not understand why Paul did and said what he did when it comes to money and remuneration. Finally, there is the further difficulty of Paul's use of technical language. Phrases like "send me on my way" or "a relationship of giving and receiving" had specific financial overtones. The former referred to providing traveling funds and supplies; the latter to a parity relationship as opposed to a patron-client relationship. Bearing these things in mind, let us consider what we find in 2 Thessalonians 3:6–10 and 1 Corinthians 9:1–18, two texts on pastoral remuneration.

There were both socially elite and nonelite Christians in Thessalonike, and Paul was not at all happy that some of the nonelite had been idle, expecting to be someone's client so they would not have to do any sort of strenuous work. We are not talking here about poor people who are beggars. We are talking about people whom patrons would see as worthy clients, people with prospects and abilities but without a patrician or an elite heritage. Freedpersons who had done reasonably well in business would be a good example.

Paul is concerned that such behavior on the part of Christians is a terrible witness to the world. But by the same token he is not happy with the business-as-usual approach of patrons, including Christian patrons, who expect to enlist their fellow Christians in entangling alliances. In some cases there were Christians who were clients of non-Christian patrons who might well expect them to undertake activities deleterious to their spiritual well-being (such as attending idolatrous feasts, or offering sacrifices to the emperor). The reason Paul might well have felt some urgency about this when he wrote 2 Thessalonians is that he was apparently in Corinth, seeing firsthand the morally compromising effects of attending idol feasts on his converts there (1 Cor. 8–10). It was hard to resocialize pagans who became Christians because their previous alliances with pagan religion and pagan friends continued to enmesh them in pagan religious practices.

From stem to stern, 2 Thessalonians 3:6–12 is about work and the need of the Thessalonians to follow Paul's example on working. When he wrote 1 Thessalonians, Paul had only a suspicion about idleness in Thessalonike. By the time he wrote 2 Thessalonians, this idleness had been confirmed as a fact. Some folks are not just being idle, they are "out of order" because they are failing to follow Paul's example to serve the community in a positive way. Paul makes clear that his personal example is already part of the received tradition of this church, for as 1 Thessalonians 2:9 indicates, when Paul first came to Thessalonike he worked hard with his hands both day and night. As a missionary strategy this was particularly smart in Thessalonike and Corinth because in both these cities there was a periodic need for tents, since both cities held Olympic-style games (in Corinth they were biannual). The tents were used as temporary dwellings for those attending the games, the ancient equivalent of a cheap motel.

Paul states in 2 Thessalonians 3:9, just as explicitly as he does in 1 Corinthians, that he has the right and the authority to ask to be supported as a teacher and apostle (compare below on 1 Cor. 9:3–18, especially v. 15). But he waived that right so as not to get caught up in patronage relationships, as had various of the idle ones, "idlers," in Thessalonike. The basic principle Paul lives by are Jesus's words that "laborers deserve their food" or, put another way, "workers are worthy of their hire." Yet he knows that he also has the right to refuse to receive such support, especially if it comes with the assumptions of patronage. Paul is probably quoting a traditional saying here about "let those who will not work not eat" (cf. Gen. 3:9; Prov. 10:4).[13] He is addressing those who refuse to work.

Verse 11 involves a clever pun—the idlers are to be busy, not busybodies or sycophants sponging off others when they are perfectly capable of working. Verse 12 says that these folks must be quiet, settle down, and earn their own food to eat. This reinforces what Paul said earlier about living quietly, minding one's own business, and working with one's hands. It is telling that here Paul is not as hard on the idlers as he is on the Corinthians who are so clearly misbehaving. Here in Thessalonike shunning the idlers is advised. In Corinth, Paul will go far as to suggest excommunication.

First Corinthians 9 is not to be seen as a defense of Paul's apostolic office, but rather a plain statement that Paul has the right to be supported by his converts. This is perfectly clear from 1 Corinthians 9:4ff. The rhetorical question "Don't we have the right to food and drink?" has only one possible answer: "Of course we do." Paul then uses a series of analogies, with soldiers who have a right to expect pay, a vintner who has a right to expect to eat some of his own grapes, a goatherd who has a right to expect to drink some of the goat's milk. Then as a clincher he quotes the example about an ox having a right to eat some of the grain that it threshes (see Deut. 25:4). This is a from-the-lesser-to-the-greater kind of argument, whereby Paul is in effect saying that if even these sorts of workers have a right to expect remuneration or payback for their work, how much more should this be true for a minister of the gospel? In verse 12, however, the argument takes a turn.

After having established clearly that he has a right to be remunerated, Paul then turns around and stresses that he has a right to refuse remuneration or support of various sorts. The reason he doesn't do this in Corinth is said to be "avoidance of hindering the gospel." What is he talking about?

Paul is referring here to the culture of paid teachers/philosophers/rhetoricians who accepted patronage or payment for their proclamations or teaching, and thereby were viewed as "compromised" or "bought and paid for," likely to say anything to please the patron or the paying audience.[14] Corinth, a boomtown in the 50s AD, was a Roman colony where patronage relationships were numerous. Yet having said what he does in verse 12, Paul turns around once more and stresses again that he, like a priest or even a temple servant, has a right to share in what is offered on the altar. Verse 14 states emphatically that "the Lord has *commanded* that those who preach the gospel should get their living from the gospel."

In light of this reemphasis, the appropriate question to ask is "What then could possibly have caused Paul not to accept remuneration in Corinth?" and not "Does Paul think ministers have a right to be paid?" In other words, Paul must provide a rationale for *not* accepting remuneration, because it is ordinarily a matter of course that ministers are paid. The rationale runs along these lines. Although Paul has a right to be paid for his preaching, if he preaches and gets paid it is then a matter of services rendered and there is nothing to brag about, no reward for work that is compulsory (or owed to those who have paid). Paul, however, wants to have the honor of offering the gospel freely so he will have something to boast about.

Is this just Pauline hubris in overdrive? No, there is more to it than that. And the more can be seen in the word *hinder*. Preaching for pay will hinder the gospel of God's free grace in Corinth, and that is no good at all. Paul knows perfectly well that if he accepts payment he will be viewed as just another hired gun caught up in the reciprocity cycle, teaching or discoursing for payment in words that—while interesting—could be seen as rhetorical hyperbole or even entertainment at best. So in Corinth, he eschews his right to be remunerated for a specific reason. Like many other groups of young Gentile converts, the Corinthians had not yet grasped the concept of giving with no thought of return, or free grace, or true self-sacrifice. But in Philippi and elsewhere, it appears that the concept of grace, and free giving and receiving as opposed to payback or payoff, was understood.

It is clear from both 2 Corinthians 11:8–9 and Philippians 4:14–16 that Paul accepted money and support from congregations that *he was not presently visiting*. What are we to make of this? First, though Paul has accepted regular support from the Philippians, there is no evidence that this is the product of a patron-client relationship, like what was on offer in Corinth. Rather, Paul characterizes his relationship with the Philippians as a relationship of giving and receiving, that is, a parity relationship (see Acts 16:15; Phil. 4). Paul could receive support at a distance because there was no danger of anyone interpreting the payment as a patronage relationship. Temporary hospitality was also fine, and Paul relied on it in various cities (see, for instance, Rom. 16 for Phoebe's support, and Acts 16 for that of Lydia).

To fully understand the dynamics in this discussion, we must appreciate as well that Jews generally did not have the same disdain for manual labor that high-status Gentiles displayed. Paul saw no shame in being a leatherworker, though various of his higher-status converts may have been embarrassed by it. This makes it all the more interesting that in 1 Corinthians 9 Paul couches his discussion in language that a person of high status would use. He talks about stepping down the social ladder, consenting to be considered more vile by working with his hands, and so on. This is the talk of a high-status person who feels that he has the freedom to forego his rights as such a person, and indeed forego some of his rights as a well-educated Roman citizen. This is exactly what a verse like 1 Corinthians 9:9 suggests: Paul submitted to being a slave to all, just as his master Jesus had done, thereby deconstructing the social hierarchies at work in his culture. This must have angered or mystified some of his high-status converts in Corinth, folks like Erastus, the city treasurer mentioned in Romans 16:23.

What should we conclude from all this interesting and complex material? Can we conclude that tent-making ministry is some sort of norm that Paul requires of other ministers, including ministers who are not even remotely in the social situation Paul is responding to? Certainly not. Should we conclude that Paul, despite his protests that ministers deserve to be paid, in the end takes it all back? Again, certainly not. We have already seen how he insisted in other circumstances that the Galatians provide financial support for their local teachers. Should the practice of freely choosing to work without a salary or support be turned into some sort of norm for modern ministers, or some sort of higher calling for those who really heroically want to follow the example of Paul? Again the answer must be no, because Paul foregoes remuneration only because of the social hindrances created in Corinth by accepting patronage or support. In other circumstances he was perfectly happy to receive support, so long as it did not involve any entangling alliances that hinder the offer of the gospel freely to all. We will see this more clearly when we discuss 2 Corinthians 8–9 a bit later in this study. But at this point it seems more appropriate to turn to a discussion of what Paul has to say about the love of money, and the things money can buy.[15]

For the Love of Money and Bling

There can be little question that Paul had a strong objection to doing ministry for mercenary reasons. The use of godliness for financial gain is something he repeatedly warns against: it is a characteristic or the telltale sign that one is dealing with a false teacher. We see this sort of critique of false teachers in 1 Timothy 6:2–5, and it leads to one of the more important discussions about money in the New Testament, found in 1 Timothy 6:6–10. But bear in mind that the context is a discussion about the traits of false teachers and how to recognize them.

Paul warns in 1 Timothy 6:6 about the dangers of avarice, and he does so by mentioning a principle he has enunciated before in Philippians 4:13—godliness with self-sufficiency is great gain (cf. 1 Tim. 4:8). Thus Paul in a sense affirms that there is great *profit* in true religion, but not of the sort the false teachers have in mind. A great deal has been made of Paul's use of *autarkeias*, which is a key term in Cynic and Stoic thought. It refers to the ideal of being self-sufficient or independent. Its literal meaning is "self-rule" or "self-sufficiency" (cf. 2 Cor. 12:9, where indeed it means sufficiency).[16] Some therefore translate the word as "contentment" here to distinguish what Paul is teaching from Cynic-Stoic teaching, not least because Paul believes in God-sufficiency, not self-sufficiency. And contentment is a possible meaning of the term.

According to this line of reasoning, Paul here is referring to someone who is content with having the necessities of life and has found his or her sufficiency in God. This makes good sense. But remember that Paul is engaging in polemics, and what he is polemicizing against is a person becoming addicted to desires and cravings that in fact run—and even ruin—a person's life. He is talking about a person who is out of control or lacking self-control. Such a person is dependent on the next fix, in this case of money or profit, to feed that need. Paul contrasts such a person, which according to him false teachers are like, to a person who is not a slave to their cravings, but rather is happy with having their basic needs met. Here we have an enthymeme, a syllogism with a suppressed premise (see 3 below). We can lay it out as follows:

1. People with corrupt minds (addicted to arguing, made sick by controversies) think religion or godliness is a means of financial profit.[17]
2. But in the process they themselves are deprived or robbed of the truth.
3. [The end result is the opposite of their aim.]
4. For paradoxically it is true that godliness or true religion with self-rule/independence is greatly profitable, though not in the way "such people" have in mind.
5. Because we brought nothing into this world and can take nothing out of it when we leave.

The mature Christian is not enslaved to one passion or another, in this case the passion for money or profit. Independence is contrasted with slavery here. More to the point, godliness and independence or self-control are contrasted with ungodly desires such as avarice, which leads to slavery and the manipulative use of religion to feed greed's addictive hunger or pining. A person who is truly godly is free from—or at least not enslaved to—such addictions. In all of this Paul is drawing on Hellenistic ideas but giving them a Christian spin. He does not agree with the Stoic notion of self-sufficiency, but he does believe that true religion sets a person free from various addictions and cravings.

Independence from the desire for riches and possessions and luxury is based on the premise that we didn't bring anything with us when we came into the world and we can't take anything with us when we leave this world. Again a popular maxim is likely being cited, which is not intended to be overpressed but to help provide a warrant for the enthymeme here. We note the parallel in Job 1:21: "I came naked from my mother's womb and naked I shall return," or more closely the Septuagint version of Ecclesiastes 5:14: "As he came from his mother's womb he shall go again, naked as he came and shall take nothing from his toil, which he may carry away in his hand."[18] The point is that we don't really own the things we have in this world. They are not so much possessions as things we hold in trust as stewards for the real owner, God.

We should not try to find our sufficiency or worth in things that do not bring us into the world and give us life, and will not in the end make death avoidable or get us to heaven. As we have noted earlier, it would not have been obvious to all pagans that "you can't take it with you," because many ancient religions did believe that at death one could take things into the afterlife. Verse 8 further emphasizes the point by indicating that we should be content with sustenance and a "covering," which could refer to clothing or to a roof over one's head.[19]

"But those desiring/wishing to be rich [it does not say they are already rich] fall into a serious temptation and snare, desiring much that is senseless and harmful, and in the end plunges one into endless ruin and eternal destruction" (v. 9). Notice the similarity between the phrase "wishing to be rich" and "wishing to be teachers of the law" (1:7). This rhetorical effect or echo suggests that Paul is referring to the same people with both phrases. We may compare the teaching about the rich man and Lazarus (Luke 18) here. Such teaching would be unneeded if there were no high-status persons in the congregation who had wealth that might enrich the coffers of the false teachers. This is the same kind of warning we find, for example, in 1 Peter 5:2, where not false teachers but actual elders in the congregations are strictly warned against being "money-grubbers," as Craig Blomberg comments: "At the very least this implies that Christian leaders should not be motivated to minister by the thought of remuneration or any particular level of payment."[20]

124

Verse 10 must be carefully translated since it is the most often quoted and misquoted line from the Pastoral Epistles.[21] In the Jewish moral tradition it was not uncommon to speak of root vices. For example, Philo speaks of desire, inequality, pride, and falsehood as vices that spawn other vices.[22] Our text says that the love of money (not money itself) is *a* root (not *the* root) of all sorts of evil (not all evil). Paul is not saying that greed or money is the origin of all evils in the world.

Here again we seem to be dealing with a common maxim. Bion the philosopher says, "Love of money is the mother-city of all evils."[23] It is noteworthy that there was a frequent criticism of Sophists, and indeed all sorts of for-hire teachers and rhetors and philosophers, that they taught in order to become wealthy.[24] Thus the false teachers are slotted into this category of teacher. It is also noteworthy that Jesus critiqued such teachers when he warned his followers to beware of scribes (theological teachers who are experts in the law) who bilk wealthy widows (Mark 12:38–40). One wonders if there is such a connection between the false teachers and the widows, perhaps especially the younger ones in the Pastorals. Here again the maxim serves as the warrant or clincher in the argument that proves the point. This same maxim crops up in a general application in Hebrews 13:5a, where we hear the Pauline advice reiterated: "Keep your lives free from the love of money and be content with what you have."[25]

It is the *attitude* towards money that is being critiqued in this passage. If we love things like money and use people to acquire these things, we have exactly reversed the way God intends for us to operate. Things are not capable of love or carrying on a loving relationship with a person. Such possessiveness is in the end a form of idolatry and of trying to find our life, support, and sufficiency in something other than God. This part of the discourse most resembles the Lukan form of Jesus's teaching on the foolishness and dangers of the love of money (see Luke 6:20, 24; 9:23–25; 12:22–34; 14:25–33; 16:13). We could even see Luke 12:15, 21 as commentary on this discussion: "Take heed and beware of all avarice; for a person's life does not consist in the abundance of his possessions . . . so is he who lays up treasure for himself and is not rich toward God."

Paul adds that this sort of sick love has led some away from the faith. They are, in essence, like a creature that has impaled itself on a spit over an open fire, causing itself endless agony. Once again the theme of apostasy surfaces, possibly even with an allusion here to hell and eternal destruction. It is noteworthy that there is a stress in this section as elsewhere in this letter on the connection between intellectual error and moral deterioration. Paul characterizes greedy persons as being both mentally and morally unwell.

We can now turn to a second passage in 1 Timothy, where Paul doesn't speak against the dangers of money but of what we now call bling. Certainly 1 Timothy 2:8–15 is one of the most controversial of all Pauline texts. For our purposes, though, we need not focus on questions of gender hierarchy raised in this text.

The passage begins in verse 8 with a reprimand of men in worship. They are to lift up hands in prayer without anger or argument. This suggests a situation where men are vying for the privilege of praying in the congregation. (In this or in other regards, there is perhaps some sort of honor and shame rivalry at work.) This instruction is a continuation of the previous remarks on offering prayer for all people, including rulers. Notice the reference to "in every place," which seems to indicate every meeting place or house church. Standing (the normal Jewish prayer posture) and raising hands in prayer is a practice regularly referred to in earlier and contemporary Jewish sources (Exod. 9:29; Ps. 27:2; Lam. 3:41; 1 Kings 8:22, 54; Neh. 8:6; Isa. 1:15).[26] Open hands were a sign of petition or of reaching out to God in need.

The hands are characterized as holy hands, and presumably this is seen as the opposite of hands lifted in anger. The phrase "holy hands" is not uncommon. For example, in Josephus we find the phrase "uplifting pure hands,"[27] and in Seneca, "to raise pure hands to heaven."[28] Holiness excludes angry, contentious behavior, especially in worship. (Notice how in Titus 1:7 the overseer is expected to be a person who is not quick to get angry.) We may compare texts like 1 Peter 3:7 and James 1:19–20, which indicate that anger gets in the way of righteousness, and will inhibit or interfere with one's prayers. The contentious situation reflected in this verse is likely related to the problems of the false teachers (cf. 1 Tim. 1:3; 4:7; 6:3–4, 20; 2 Tim. 2:16–17, 23), some of whom may well have been women or at least had influenced some high-status women, hence the reprimand in the following verses. We may suppose, since there are false teachers in this social context, that there are some divisive forces at work in these house churches. Paul is trying to mend that situation.

We must take seriously the word *hōsautōs* which begins verse 9, and means "likewise." This suggests that Paul is envisioning women praying as well as men, and he wishes them to do it with the same decorum or holiness the men must exercise. The word *katastolē* refers to demeanor in both its inward and outward sense.[29] Women are to be clothed outwardly in modest and nondistracting clothing and inwardly in self-respect and modesty. The phrase *meta aidous* normally means "with (self-) respect," although there are texts where it can have the sense of religious awe.[30] Philo tells us that this was a virtue expected typically of women.[31] In this culture, modesty, self-control, piety, and self-respect are virtues regularly touted and attributed to women.

If we do not read verse 9 as a continuation of the instructions about prayer in verse 8, then the reference to women's adornment seems to be an unmotivated digression. John Chrysostom in fact concluded, in my judgment rightly, that we must insert the main verb again so that the text reads in essence "likewise [I desire] women also to pray being adorned in modesty and holy fashion." Chrysostom puts it this way: "Equally with men, women are called to approach God without wrath or doubting, lifting up holy hands. . . . Paul however requires something more of women, that they adorn themselves 'in modest apparel, with self respect and sobriety.'"[32]

Verse 9 continues the topic of dress and jewelry, and there is good reason to think Paul that has something particular in mind. James Hurley writes, "He refers . . . to the elaborate hair-styles which were fashionable among the wealthy, and [perhaps] also to the styles worn by courtesans. The sculpture and the literature of the period make it clear that women often wore their hair in enormously elaborate arrangements with braids and curls interwoven or piled high like towers and decorated with gems and/or gold and/or pearls. The courtesans wore their hair in numerous small pendant braids with gold droplets or pearls or gems every inch or so, making a shimmery screen of their locks."[33] We should envision the scene as an evening Christian worship meeting in a relatively small space, with many lamps lit. In this situation hairstyles dotted with reflective items (such as gold or pearls) would be a regular distraction from the proper focus of worship. The advice given here seems to have been part of the general ethical code suggested for Christian women of some status. For instance, in 1 Peter 3:3–4 we hear wives warned that their beauty should not come from their bling and apparel, outward adornment—braided hair, gold jewelry, fine clothes—but from their inner spirit, which should be both gentle and quiet.

Paul then is not merely arguing here for modest apparel, but against ostentatious, flashy, and distracting apparel. Such apparel goes against the rules of modesty, discretion, propriety, and sobriety that were to apply to everyone in worship, especially when meeting in close quarters. To some degree this critique of women's apparel is like the critique we find in Juvenal or Plutarch, but we can also point to a Jewish saying like: "accordingly order your wives and daughters not to adorn their heads and their appearances so as to deceive men's sound minds."[34] We should add that only women who had slaves or hairdressers to help them, which is to say they were women of higher status, could have the sort of elaborate hairdos Paul refers to here. Once more we have the stress on *sōphrosynē*. This Greek term suggests prudence, temperance, discretion, soundness of judgment, and self-control, the Greek ideal of behavior.[35] Women are called at the end of this verse to do what is fitting for women who profess to worship God through good works. Fitting deportment in worship was crucial for both men and women not only because other Christians would be watching but also since this was the time when they might invite non-Christian friends to come and be a part of the Christian meeting (see, for example, 1 Cor. 14:23).

The Pauline Collection for Jerusalem

Before we conclude this chapter something must be said about the collection for the poor saints in Jerusalem, which was a cause célèbre for Paul, particularly in the early part of his ministry. We find the commission for this collection already in Galatians 2:10, the first reference to what is undertaken in 1 Corinthians 16:1–2 (where Paul says that money should be set aside on the day of worship, the first day of the week, for this collection). Another reference appears in 2 Corinthians 8–9, describing how the Philippians and others have been contributing and the Corinthians needed to get on with it, and then yet a further reference in Romans 15:25–28, just before Paul heads to Jerusalem in about AD 57 to deliver this collection for those suffering from famine and food shortage in Jerusalem. Acts 20:4 probably hints that Paul took representatives of the donating churches with him when he finally took the funds to the elders in Jerusalem. In other words, the one time Paul really talks about money that would be given to a church or church group is when he is concerned about collecting funds for the poor and indigent in the church in Jerusalem. Even 1 Corinthians 16:1–2 is not a general remark about setting aside money for the weekly collection for one's own house church.

If we read carefully all of the passages listed in this paragraph we clearly see how far the typical modern Western church has departed from early church practices. On average, most American churches spend about 90 percent of their budgets or more on the upkeep of their own facilities and the funding of ministries that benefit themselves. Paul by contrast encourages his converts in Turkey and Greece to give donations to a church overseas, whose members only Paul himself really knew! Paul saw such giving as a way of binding the church of Gentiles and Jews together into one family.

It is to this more global vision of what the church should do with its funds, even when it is just thinking about "doing good to the household of faith," to which Paul calls us all. We need to lift up our eyes and act upon what we know about our starving brothers and sisters in Darfur and other places overseas. It is in fact a sign of real Christian maturity and faith in times of crisis that a person will be especially concerned about others even when one is feeling the pinch oneself. In a time when people are hoarding resources, if the church is seen to be taking care of its own and self-sacrificially caring for others as well, the witness of Christ will become plain to one and all. What we do with our money in crisis is often the clearest expression of who we really are, and in whom we really trust.

And So?

What have we learned from our all-too-cursory treatment of some of the relevant Pauline material? We have learned that Paul deliberately inculcated an approach to Christian life that does not involve conspicuous consumption, ostentatious dress, and a lavish lifestyle. Rather, he inculcated a lifestyle of godliness with contentment. The lifestyles of the rich and famous are seen as a hindrance to Christian moral integrity, not to mention a theft of food and clothing from the poor. Greed, the love of money, is seen as a root of all kinds of evil and is to be avoided at all costs by the Christians (especially by the Christian minister, for Paul is addressing his coworker Timothy particularly in 1 Timothy 6). Equally to be avoided is a mercenary motive for undertaking ministry.

Paul believes in hard work wholeheartedly—indeed he frequently brags about his work regimen (2 Corinthians 11, for example). He reprimands high-status persons in the culture who look down their noses at manual labor. And Paul has nothing but correction for the idlers who refuse to work, saying that if that is their posture then Christians should shun them. They should not be allowed to partake of the fellowship meals as a rule: let those who will not work not eat! Free grace doesn't mean a free ride or welcoming freeloaders. (Here Paul particularly has in mind those who are likely to become clients of well-known patrons.)

It is clear that we cannot really understand what Paul has to say about ministry and remuneration unless we understand the tricky situation at work in a patronage and reciprocity culture. In general Paul believes a congregation has an obligation to pay its teachers or ministers, but the minister may exercise the right or freedom to refuse pay. This, however, does not get the church off the hook when it comes to its obligation to offer remuneration for ministerial work. Paul in fact believes that Jesus commanded that ministers should be paid for the proclamation of the gospel. But entangling alliances and compromising social relationships must be avoided, and the gospel must not be seen to be an example of flattery or mere rhetoric offered by a for-hire sophist.

Paul is not an advocate of what modern persons call tent-making ministry, if by that we mean that church planters or missionaries should expect to have to work on the side or raise their own support while doing ministry. Again, they *may* do so, as Paul did in Corinth and apparently in Thessalonike. But 1 Corinthians 9 rules out the view that they *necessarily should or must do so*. If they choose to go this route, it needs to be for the right reasons, not because it assumes that the New Testament suggests we should not have paid ministers. To the contrary, argues Paul, churches should expect to pay their ministers. What is interesting and ironic about all this is that the very document that is assumed to most argue against paid ministers (1 Corinthians) is the document that provides the clearest rationale for why congregations should expect to pay a Paul or a Peter or a Timothy or a Titus, or whoever their local teachers (see Galatians 6) might be.

8

John of Patmos and a News Flash for the Merchants and Mr. 666

Money often costs too much.
—Ralph Waldo Emerson

One of the real problems for Christians, perhaps especially in North America, is the tendency to separate matters of church and state, faith and business, inner attitudes and outward behavior, all in a way that can lead to failure to integrate our beliefs with our behavior. Sometimes we are guilty of failing to see the spiritual implications of certain approaches to material things and prosperity, even as we so often evaluate who we are on the basis of what we have.

Despite the numerous scriptural warnings about the deleterious effects of wealth and prosperity on one's spiritual life, we still continue to strive for material success, go to motivational seminars, and live lives of conspicuous consumption. But in addition to the failure to see the interplay between the spiritual and the material, there is an almost equal failure in our culture to think systematically about the problem. Christians tend to privatize their ethics just as they privatize their property, and so assume that the root of the problem when we are dealing with the sins of greed and material excess is always within the private individual. But suppose the problems are not just matters of personal imbalance or the lusts of the heart? Suppose one of the main sources of the problem is the culture itself in which we are immersed, and the economic and political systems that shape and determine so much about that culture?

To his credit John of Patmos addresses both the individual and cultural dimensions of the problem of materialism. We turn now to his book of Revelation. We look first at Revelation 2–3, where John deals with the spiritual and material issues in tandem. Then we turn to Revelation 17, where he foretells the coming judgment on greedy merchants who have gotten in bed with the superpower known as Rome, and will share its fall and destruction when it goes down for the count.

Revelation 2–3: Spiritually Rich and Materially Poor, Spiritually Poor and Materially Rich

John was a prophet, even when he drew on epistolary and rhetorical conventions, and so not surprisingly there is a decidedly prophetic character to the letters to the seven churches in Revelation 2–3. In fact there is a clearly demarcated prophetic character to the oracles to these churches. John's address to each of the churches features a shared prophetic pattern: (1) an introductory commissioning word; (2) a middle or central section; and (3) a double conclusion involving a call for vigilance and a saying about overcoming adversity.

Notice that there is a citation formula here, "thus says" (*tade legei*), after which the exalted Christ speaks in each case. The content of each oracle that follows the citation formula in its central or middle "I know" part varies according to the situation of each church. The exhortative nature of the central section of these prophecies is clear and the often strongly negative tone reminds us that Christian prophets and seers like John saw themselves as having a role similar to that played by Old Testament prophets. They were the guardians and protectors of Christian behavior and beliefs. They could also be prosecutors of a lawsuit (so to speak) on behalf of God's covenant, only in this case they spoke for the new covenant. We may conjecture that there must have been a dearth of leadership in these churches, which in turn necessitated prophetic intervention by John. Prophets and seers could be seen as crisis intervention specialists, especially when there was a power or leadership vacuum.

It is crucial to note at the outset that John would have us understand that it is the exalted Christ who is offering these exhortations and commands, not merely John of Patmos. So while we tend to call this material the teachings of John of Patmos, he would tell us that he is merely pronouncing the "Amen" as the messenger conveying what the ascended Christ has conveyed to him in a vision.

The church in Smyrna (modern day Izmir, Turkey) is said in Revelation 2:9 to be suffering material poverty. And yet the church is said to be *spiritually* rich. (This is the direct opposite of what is said later about the church in Laodicea.) It is entirely possible that the poverty of Christians in Smyrna resulted from their refusal to participate in the guild system, which in turn locked them out of numerous jobs. Guilds were in some respects the ancient equivalent of unions, and in order to participate in some trades one had to be a guild member. The problem for the Christian was that guilds required participation in various sorts of pagan religious ceremonies. Smyrna was the second city in the region that embraced the imperial cult,[1] and one's civic virtue was evidenced by participation in the rites of this cult, which included forms of emperor worship and even sacrifice to the emperor. The guilds were some of the leading civic organizations participating in such rites. It must also be remembered that the Emperor Domitian demanded that he be recognized as *Deus et Dominus Noster*, "our Lord and our God." Notice, however, that John seems to blame some Jews in Smyrna for difficulties faced by Christians in that city. Whatever the source of the troubles, the result was the material—though not the spiritual—poverty of some Christians.

There are of course debates about the relationship between spiritual growth and material well-being. Perhaps the simplest and most obvious thing to note is that poor people are not under the delusion of a false sense of security that material wealth can bring. If they are at all religious, they know their need for outside help, indeed their need for divine help. Then too when a person has been stripped of all worldly goods or at least all reserves, most will see themselves as being in a crisis and turn to whatever ultimate source of succor they believe in. Crisis, including an economic crisis, can indeed deepen someone's faith and dependence on God. So while it may come as a surprise to some prosperity preachers, poverty can actually help one's prayer and spiritual life. And at least for a time it can be seen as a blessing from God that has driven the person into the arms of the Almighty. By the same token, material success can just as well be seen as a temptation from the Dark One meant to destroy one's soul. John of Patmos knew this, and he speaks more directly about it in Revelaton 3:14–22, to which we now turn.

The letter to the church at Laodicea is perhaps the most famous of all the letters to the seven churches because of the image of Christ making a "house call" to a church that has gone astray. Laodicea was a wealthy town, with a famous medical school and numerous banks. As recent excavations have shown, the city had colonnaded streets and enormous theaters and stadiums. It lay only six miles from Hierapolis, where the wealthy came (and still come) to the hot springs for rest and restoration. Despite the material wealth of the Christians in Laodicea's church, there is absolutely no commendation for this church, though there is for each of the other six churches John addresses. The Christians at Laodicea are said to brag that they are rich and have no obvious needs. And this has led to complacency and a brackish, tepid spirituality.

The Laodiceans are faulted for being neither hot nor cold, and so they are unpalatable to Christ. What has been totally lost in the rush to material success and satisfaction is any real sense of self-knowledge. The Laodiceans have become spiritually bankrupt and naked, *and they don't even know it.* No self-help seminars are going to rescue them. Christ's personal visit and application of the "cure" is depicted as the only thing that can help them now. Here we are at the heart of one of the main problems for Christians in the prosperous West. Too often we are not self-aware of the dangers prosperity poses to our spiritual life. The only good news is that Christ calls this church to repentance, which reveals that there is still some hope for it. But each individual in the church must respond to the call for repentance from a lifestyle of opulence and excess.

John often uses irony and contrast to point out the difficulties facing one or another church, and the letter to the Laodiceans is no exception. One might think that material success would give a person time and opportunity to focus more on one's spiritual life, but it had not worked that way in Laodicea. Caught up in the dominant milieu of their culture, high-status Christians had become high rollers, and did not realize that they were not merely gambling away their spiritual lives, but indeed were in danger of jettisoning their eternal lives as well.

We might think that as Americans we are immune to these sorts of problems since we have a separation of church and state, whereas in that world religion and politics, spirituality and material reality, were all blended together. But in fact, the bifurcation of the spiritual and the material in our culture has led to blindness about the dangers the Bible warns against when it comes to wealth and prosperity. It has led to a failure to connect the spiritual and the material, and to self-justifying talk as if success must be a sign of blessing from God. Christians, like the culture around us, have become blind to the deadening effect of materialism. If we wish to see the ultimate outcome of greed and the relentless pursuit of wealth and prosperity, we don't need to read the famous story of *Silas Marner* or listen to other folk tales. All we need to do is consider in some depth the descriptions in Revelation 17–18 about the demise of the Roman Empire and its economic sycophants. (And I stress at this point that John is not the only one who suggested such ideas. We have seen them already in the teachings of Jesus and James.)

Revelation 17–18: The Harlot and Her Wardrobe

The great merit of J. Nelson Kraybill's detailed study of Roman economics and the book of Revelation is that he demonstrates how economic hardship was intertwined with any attempt by a late first-century Christian to resist the rising tide of idolatrous influences in the culture, particularly the emperor cult.[2] John warns his converts about the dangers of getting into bed economically with the emperor and empire by telling a tale of two cities: Rome and the new Jerusalem. He serves up a rhetorical comparison by contrast, meant to help his audience disengage and disentangle themselves from the idolatrous economics of the emperor cult. John's contrast could hardly be starker: a beautiful, radiant bride (the new Jerusalem) and a harlot decked out with way too much bling (Rome). The point of the portraits is to encourage the audience to resist vice and pursue virtue. And here virtue entails disengagement from immoral and religiously dangerous business practices.

Like a Wall Street analyst who is uncannily correct in predicting a market crash, John portrays in advance the fall of Rome and its economic allies all in an hour. Unlike assumptions made in our day, the economic downturn is seen by John to be a direct result of the judgment of God—indeed, it is part and parcel of God's judgment on Rome itself.

The opening salvo is impressive. In Revelation 17:1–2 John depicts a harlot who sits on many waters, with whom the cities of the Mediterranean world have fornicated. A multinational empire run from Rome has wooed and won multinational merchants of various cities. With the images of fornication and drunkenness, John stresses the deleterious effects of the imperial city and culture on lesser powers and persons. If a person accepts Rome's patronage and becomes her slave (or sycophantic client), he or she will go down with the mother ship when it sinks.

What is perhaps most unsettling here is that John accuses the clients of worshiping Rome herself, doubtless in the guise of the goddess Roma (who was pictured on the religious emblem of the city). Any time someone gives a country unconditional and unquestioned allegiance one has committed idolatry, and John is accusing these merchants of selling their souls for profits and prosperity. John's caricature of Rome is meant to demythologize both the city and its civic religion, and help his audience resist the influence of the imperial cult as well.

John says that there is a mystery to iniquity. How could something so big, so powerful, so successful in some ways, so opulent or beautiful be so wicked and soul-destroying? How could this happen if God is not on their side? The Roman Empire, like various modern ones, believed that bigger is better, that more impressive means more important, and that "succeeding" cures all ills. And it made the huge mistake of wedding the socioeconomic system to both the political and religious systems. It was literally one-stop shopping: worship the emperor and respect the empire, get favorable trade agreements, and prosper. It was simple—and it was wicked, a form of idolatry.

But John is not just tilting at a distant Roman windmill. At the time of his writing of Revelation, he is in exile for something he said and did in Asia. Whatever it was it surely included the critiquing of local high-status elites and the way they had sucked up to the emperor and empire in order to live long and prosper. It seems that he critiqued the local populace in general and not just their officials. He made himself enough of a local nuisance to warrant exile to the penal colony on Patmos.

Revelation 18 is a remarkable display of rhetorical power, meant to send chills down the spine of anyone who would sell their soul for profits and success, especially by means of government contracts, so to speak. It turns out that not just the kings of the earth but the merchants, the sea captains, and the sailors had all gotten on board the good ship Rome. And all would sink with it as well, in John's vision. The suddenness and unexpectedness of the demise is stressed throughout this chapter.

But let me be clear about what John is and is not saying. John is not against commerce itself. But he calls his audience to "come out from them" (18:4), meaning that he is warning his audience to sever or avoid economic ties (with the "beast" being the empire, and Mr. 666 being the emperor himself, in this case Domitian), not least because one then becomes enmeshed in direct idolatry and moral compromise. Such enmeshment involves an unholy alliance with the emperor, despite the fact that he is not God and he has no divine clothes.[3] Let me stress that the critique here is not merely of false religion or immorality in general but more specifically of greed and materialism, the wrong sort of orientation towards the good things of this world.

Notice the complaint in 18:3: the merchants have become rich from the power of Rome's luxury, which in turn depends on Rome's desire for luxury. Greed is at the root of the matter, and greed is one of the vices most frequently condemned in the New Testament. The point of the long and detailed lists of imports is to show just how sick the great city of Rome is, how deeply sunk in greed are its elites. John has nothing but condemnation for such an orientation in life. Jewels and pearls and gold and ivory are *not* necessities for the truly good life. They are only and always luxury items, and it is quite specifically luxury that John is condemning here. He speaks against the lust for luxury and the way it causes people to compromise their morals and literally "lose their religion," if they had any good religion to begin with. And this brings us to the issue of slavery.

There were perhaps sixty million slaves (from one-third to one-half of the population) in the Roman Empire at the time John was writing. Slaves did the work for the wealthy. They did not have to be paid properly; they staffed the brothels and performed in the theaters and arenas. Slaves even educated their masters' children, sometimes ran their businesses, and more. We should not make the mistake of thinking of purely agricultural slavery or of all slaves being illiterate and poor. Most of the slaves came from the conquests of the Roman armies and often the captives who ended up on the auction block included well-educated and high-status persons. Almost anyone—however wealthy or educated—could become a slave of a Roman if he or she had the misfortune of living in a place conquered by Rome.

There are, of course, dimensions to the situation in the Roman world that have no direct analogs today in the West, but one is immediately struck by the similarities of hiring illegal aliens and paying them poorly to do low-status, dirty work.[4] Or we might think of American companies rushing to outsource production of their goods in China or other countries where cheap labor forces can be had. And in fact the ultimate cause of this modern development is twofold: the Western lust for cheap goods even at the expense of forcing their own neighbors to close their local businesses; the never-ending desire for more and higher profits. There is then the very same soul sickness in our culture that John so vividly depicts in Rome and its allies. Its name is greed—the lust for prosperity, wealth, luxury.

And So?

In sum, we can speak of John's critique as being one that applies to both the individual and the collective whole of society. He isn't just interested in pointing out internal and personal causes of the demise of a Christian life and its spiritual substance, though when he does focus on that he minces no words in declaring that wealth and materialism can ruin a Christian life. Still, John was not sent into exile for counseling individual Christians to de-enculturate themselves from the materialistic values of their culture and contemporaries.

In all likelihood it was precisely the sort of critique we find in Revelation 17–18 that got John into trouble. John was an equal opportunity critic of both the micro and macro causes of spiritual problems. His call to "come out from them" meant not merely giving up materialism and greed, but ending business as usual and facing the changes that would likely come with the application of Christian ethics to business life.

Sin is not just a personal and private matter. It is woven into the very fabric of the fallen world and all its institutions, be they political, economic, or religious. John knew this and he was prepared to critique sin from the top down—from the heights of the seven hills of Rome where the emperor sat, to the depths of the human heart where the lust called greed and the disease called materialism reside. I suspect John's critique of our world would be equally strong and severe. Would John not look on our world and see prosperous Christians in the West who have succeeded on the backs of near slave labor, or at the expense of their neighbor, or through shady business ethics, and people have simply baptized the lifestyles of the rich and famous and called them good?

Having completed a survey of the New Testament texts on money and prosperity, it is now time to turn to an overall evaluation of the thrust and weight of the New Testament evidence and its Old Testament background. What should we really think today about money, wealth, prosperity, poverty, work, remuneration of ministers, and related matters? What would the New Testament writers say to us if they were able to speak directly to us today?

9

Towards a New Testament Theology of Money, Stewardship, and Giving

> You have reached the pinnacle of success as soon as you be-
> come uninterested in money, compliments, or publicity.
>
> —Thomas Wolfe

> Money is like manure; it's not worth a thing unless it's spread
> around encouraging young things to grow.
>
> —Thornton Wilder

In her excellent study towards the formation of a theology of possessions, giving, money, and wealth, Sondra Wheeler remarks that it is
crucial to take into account the whole of the New Testament canon,
with all its variety. One of the important reasons for a comprehensive
approach is that if we take very situation-specific injunctions and
attempt to universalize them, we quickly run into conflict with other
New Testament imperatives that are equally important. For instance,
imagine someone who takes Luke 12:33 ("sell your possessions and
give to the poor") to be incumbent on all Christians in every situation,
literally follows it, and then meets the commandment "do not neglect
hospitality" (Heb. 13:2). If one has no home or possessions, how can

one offer hospitality?[1] In other words, a canonical approach suggests that there must be a balance in the way we evaluate the evidence, not universalizing a calling or demand that may be meant for particular persons, living in particular circumstances and places.

Wheeler is also correct in her assertion that much of the orientation towards money and wealth in the New Testament carries forward Old Testament assumptions about the subject. First is the assumption that God is the creator and owner of all things. Second, God's creatures are not owners but only stewards of material things, even when one has worked for them and earned them in one sense. Third, we find in the Old Testament the conviction that human beings are fallen, and that the internal battles with things like greed are ongoing; one cannot afford to be naïve about that. And finally, in light of the multitudinous warnings in the Bible about wealth (repeatedly associated with idolatry and apostasy), a believer must be wary and take a cautious approach to the issue of money and possessions.

Not for nothing does Isaiah prophesy that the luxury and pride of the daughters of Zion will lead not merely to complacency and spiritual degradation but to their downfall (Isa. 3:16–24). We can also point to Amos, who vividly critiques the idle wealthy and warns that they shall be the first ones to go into exile (Amos 6:4–7); and to God himself, who complains that when he did bless Israel with prosperity she became rebellious and idolatrous, "forgetting the God who gave you birth" (Deut. 32:10–18).

Prosperous modern Christians ignore these warnings at our peril, for our fallen attitudes about wealth and prosperity are no different from those of ancient Israel. It is precisely these texts that remind us that we cannot simply focus on the Old or New Testament texts that say that sometimes wealth can be a reward and blessing from God for good honest labor. We must meditate on the whole witness of the canon. And herein lies a huge part of the problem. When we treat, say, certain verses in Proverbs in isolation from what the rest of the canon says, and without an understanding of how proverbs and maxims work, then we do not merely mistake the part for the whole but we even violate the character of the part—which says that sometimes material things are a blessing from God and a reward for good hard honest labor.

Furthermore, when we turn to the New Testament itself, the warnings about wealth as a potential spiritual stumbling block only intensify. Let me say that again: the New Testament, if anything, is harder on the assumptions of the health-and-wealth gospel than the Old Testament.[2] It is the New Testament that stresses a person is not to store up his or her treasure on earth, and urges that the love of money is a root of all kinds of evil. And then too, the most one can get out of the "seek ye first . . . and all these things will be added" texts is that believers are encouraged to rely on God, not their brokers, for the provision of their basic needs (Acts 4:34; Matt. 6:33; Luke 6:31; 2 Cor. 9:10–11).

These texts do reassure that God can and will give his people what is necessary to sustain an obedient life, though there will undoubtedly be times of testing. We have also repeatedly noted that when the Bible actually does say something about God blessing a person with material prosperity, usually the text says that God does this for the righteous, which is to say those who are likely to use such resources in a good and godly way. For others, ruled by their errant desires and lusts, prosperity is seen more as a temptation and a snare than a blessing. In any case, the New Testament is very clear that the goal of the Christian life is not success or prosperity, but godliness with contentment, which Paul stresses is the greatest gain of all.

There is a balance to what is being said in the New Testament. Despite the opinions of many of the church fathers, the New Testament does not urge us all to asceticism. Nor does it suggest that material poverty is inherently a more spiritual condition than wealth, though clearly there are fewer material encumbrances and stumbling blocks to a healthy relationship with God for the poor. Wheeler helpfully puts the matter as follows:

> And while material wealth may no longer be attributed [in the NT] to the virtues of the rich or taken as a sign of God's approval, neither is it attributed to the Devil. There is in the NT no pure asceticism that deprecates material reality as intrinsically evil [unlike in Gnostic thought], and no talk of a mystical ascent to God by means of a withdrawal from bodily reality. The dangers of distraction and entanglement, of misplaced trust and loyalty that inhere in ownership are all brought forward, but there is no repudiation of material goods as such. The disciples may be directed to sell their possessions and give them to the poor; they are never directed simply to throw them away. The necessity and goodness of wealth as a resource for the meeting of human needs are affirmed; and as we have seen, the same epistles which condemn greed as idolatrous can commend provision for oneself and one's family as a duty.[3]

To this last point we could add that there is also strong emphasis on the right of ministers to be paid for their efforts and supported by those they serve. The principle of workers being worthy of their hire is in some ways the flip side of saying "let those who will not work not eat." Work is valued, and is expected to be remunerated, unless the worker chooses to offer it for free. This is as true of the minister as of any Christian in the New Testament.

Though most of the New Testament places an emphasis on the problems of the individual and on individual responsibility when it comes to wealth and sacrifice, nevertheless we saw in our last chapter that the author of Revelation begins to push us in the direction of thinking about systemic evil, asking pointed and hard questions about the economic structures of the society in which we are enmeshed and engulfed. Wheeler has very adequately articulated some of the justice questions we should raise (see also John Wesley's sermon "The Use of Money" in appendix 2).

Wheeler suggests that we ask a number of questions. First, to what extent is the wealth of modern Christians the product of coercive, exploitive, immoral labor, management, or marketing practices? Second, to what extent does our material prosperity or its perpetuation depend upon and help to perpetuate unjust structures and institutions in society and the world? Third, can we actually defend the work we do as a moral practice that contributes to human good and is compatible with the command to love one's neighbor, even the enemy, and serve them as well? Fourth, are we unnecessarily holding on to assets that could be used to alleviate the plight of the poor and the needy? Are we able to defend the share of benefits we have and burdens we undertake as both just and equitable? Fifth, how do more well-off Christians make use of social power? Do they use it to create unfair advantages or privileged access to yet more resources and wealth for themselves?[4] To these questions we should add: To what extent is it even possible for a prosperous Christian to hear a call to divestiture, or even the call to simplify one's lifestyle and give more to the needy? One of the great problems with the prosperity gospel is that it removes any lingering guilt about being a conspicuous consumer and indeed aids the process of increasing spiritual deafness to the cries of the poor. It gives permission to turn off such nagging voices in one's head, or to write off poor people in general as victims of their own bad choices, laziness, or the like.

In his detailed treatment of all the biblical passages about possessions and wealth, Craig Blomberg comes to very measured and helpful conclusions especially about what the New Testament says on the matter. He is quite right that material poverty is never seen as a good thing in itself, and by the same token material possessions *can* be seen as a good gift from God meant to meet the needs of other persons. The problem is that human beings are all—without exception—fallen creatures. And the real essence of that condition is self-centeredness, which in turn leads to an infinite capacity for self-justification and rationalization of one's behavior, especially the expenditure of our so-called disposable income. This is why a good thing, namely material possessions, can simultaneously become a means of turning human hearts away from God.[5]

It is also quite true that what one does with one's money reveals where one's heart is, and whether or not that heart has been transformed when a person claims to be a Christian. As Blomberg points out, the wealthy but godly patriarchs are all depicted as having shared generously with the needy. There was a connection between their spirituality and their generosity. This makes good sense. A person who is really trusting God finds it easier to let go of material things and be motivated to generosity and kindness. If "in God we trust" is more than a motto on our coins, it means that we do not place ultimate trust in a bank account. It means we believe that God can come to our aid in the future as well as in the present, hence obviating the need to hold on to our possessions with both hands. Some of the patriarchs at least seem to have known this, even when they had become prosperous.

Blomberg goes on to stress that the New Testament suggests that certain extremes of wealth and poverty are clearly viewed as *intolerable*, though it is hard to quantify such things.[6] This conclusion comports with his further one that what the Bible is really talking about is all things in moderation, though extreme sacrifice is often encouraged and commended in specific situations. Blomberg takes Proverbs 30:8 ("Give me neither poverty nor wealth") as the source of the title for his book *Neither Wealth nor Poverty*. He sees in the way God provided daily manna for the Israelites in the wilderness a divine sanction of the principle of "enough," or moderation. This may be correct, and it is not an accident that Paul alludes to that very story when he exhorts the Corinthians to finish the job of collecting funds for the poor saints in Jerusalem.

Perhaps here it is good to reiterate what the New Testament suggests about the matter of churches "taking up collections." Paul's appeal to the Corinthians in 2 Corinthians 8–9 deserves a closer examination, but we should note from the outset that Paul is not just urging generosity in general in these chapters. He has some principles in mind. First is that persons should give according to their means (v. 11). Second, the goal here as Paul says is "not that others should be relieved while you are hard-pressed, but that there might be equality. At the present time your plenty will supply what they need, so that in turn their plenty will supply what you need. The goal is equality" (2 Cor. 8:13–14). At this juncture Paul quotes Exodus 16:15.

But what exactly is equity or equality within the body of Christ? Paul assumes that the customary system of patronage will continue, and that there will be some Christians with more, and some with fewer, possessions. He appeals to the Christian principle of generosity, but he does not suggest a foolish sacrifice. He advises giving "according to one's means." Equality here may just be another way of talking about what we saw in Acts 2, where it is said that no one should go without necessities, so that giving is done on the principle of each giving according to their means and each receiving according to their needs. On the one hand Paul clearly attempts to shame the Corinthians into action by mentioning that the Macedonian Christians, despite their extreme poverty, gave to the collection for the poor. And they gave not merely according to their ability but even beyond their ability—indeed, they asked to be benefactors of the collection. They wanted to share in Paul's ministry to the saints in Jerusalem. On the other hand Paul says that he is not in favor of some being burdened while others are eased.

It is in the context of a discussion about the collection for the saints (2 Cor. 8:9) that we hear about Jesus not only humbling himself in the sense of becoming a human being, but even taking on material poverty in order that he might gain spiritual riches for his followers. The function of this reminder is not to insist that the Corinthians all become poor like Jesus, but that they make sacrifices like Jesus did, out of a generous heart and a real concern for equity. Here Paul is urging that a reciprocity relationship be set up between two very different parts of the Christian church. For now the Jerusalem church needs material help. But Paul foresees a day when the Jerusalem church might reciprocate if a need developed in Corinth.

The phrase "give from what you have" in 2 Corinthians 8:11b is important. Paul is not asking the Corinthians to go and take out a loan in order to help. Nor is the sheer amount the crucial thing. He says that if enthusiasm and sincerity are present then any size of gift is acceptable. Here he is no doubt encouraging less well-off Christians to contribute without feeling a sense of shame about how little they can give. In an honor and shame culture, shame was often an impediment to giving by those of modest means. In 2 Corinthians 9:7, Paul stresses that each individual should decide in his or her own heart what will be given, and not do it reluctantly, for God loves a cheerful giver. Paul also suggests that such giving, which he says is like sowing, leads to a proportionate harvest—if you sow little you reap little.

Here Paul's advice is remarkably close to Aristotle's: "liberality should be evaluated on the basis of one's capital. It is not determined by how much is given but on the basis of the donor's disposition, which gives in proportion to capital."[7] The term *isotēs* (equality) is crucial here. For Aristotle this means that when a reciprocity relationship is set up that does not involve social equals, equality is achieved by the patron receiving more praise and honor whereas the client receives the goods and funds that are needed.

Paul of course believes that all people are created equal in God's image (something Aristotle would have rejected, especially when it comes to slaves), and that all in Christ are new creatures and are of equal sacred worth as redeemed persons. But the equity he discusses in 2 Corinthians 8, while perhaps based on such theological assumptions, is an equity that actually involves economics to some extent. The Corinthians have benefited from the spiritual heritage bequeathed them by the Jerusalem church and people like Paul. They can reciprocate by giving monetarily to famine relief of the saints. The quotation of Exodus 16:18 provides clarity about what Paul means by equity: no one going without in the Christian community. Paul, as we already saw in Galatians 6, felt strongly about the household of faith taking care of its own, and this involved a transnational entity called the *ekklēsia* (church) of God, not merely a local congregation.

The discussion continues in 2 Corinthians 9, adding other facets to the teaching. Paul in essence (at 9:6–11) begins to preach that God often blesses people materially in order that they may be a blessing to others. In 9:8 he enunciates a principle of "enough." His prayer is that the audience will have enough so as not to be dependent on others. The Greek word here (*autarkeia*) can mean independence, but Paul is talking about financial independence of a certain sort, a sufficiency that enables generous giving to others.

Paul's desire is that the Corinthians be free from want and the nagging dominance of the quest for life's necessities. He prays that they have enough so that there can be a "harvest of righteousness," by which he means that they may with their generosity be a blessing to other believers in need. The term *righteousness* here is almost a synonym for generosity, and thus 2 Corinthians 8–9 provides one more piece of evidence that what we do with our surplus money reveals our true character. But there is a further benefit of giving, namely that thanksgiving and praise will be given to God by those who receive what the Corinthians give. So the end result of such giving is that a good witness is borne to God before a watching world, and more Christians are actually led to praise God.

What must not be missed in the discussion of the collection is this: while it is clear that Paul does not advocate for communism of any sort, it is also clear that he does advocate for communalism, or community-ism. By this I mean that he believes the Christian community must not allow any of its members to be in want. Paul sees this as an obligation not merely within a particular congregation but as part of an empire-wide group of churches. Christians should take care of their own. Paul is not advocating that patrons stop being patrons, nor does he mean by equity that all persons have exactly the same quality and quantity of material resources. His argument is more sophisticated than that. He is interested, especially in a time of economic crisis for the Jerusalem church, in setting up reciprocity networks so that the needs of that church can be taken care of by other churches who can certainly afford to help. Notice as well the stress on not trying to create further problems by burdening the givers in order to alleviate the need of the receivers.

Paul also focuses on each individual Christian giving freely, as each has determined from a glad and generous heart. Paul believes that such giving never goes unrewarded, though often the rewards may not be monetary. It must be stressed that when Paul says "he who sows sparingly, reaps sparingly," he is not enunciating an economic theory. The discussion here involves both spiritual and material matters. The two are intertwined, and it would be a huge mistake to extract the saying from its context and assume that it means that a Christian who gives huge sums of money is thereby guaranteed a huge *financial* return. This conclusion is positively ruled out by the example of Jesus given at the beginning of the discussion (2 Cor. 8:9). Jesus, who had all the riches of heaven, gave everything, became poor, and did not receive back a huge monetary return. Instead, he made available to others great spiritual riches—a true example of giving without any thought of return.

Material giving *may* be recompensed by spiritual rewards of various sorts. And the spiritual giving of the Jerusalem church should result at a minimum in the Gentile churches taking care of them materially when they are in need due to the famine. This is one aspect of the equality Paul refers to here.

Likewise, when Jesus promises Peter many houses and brothers in the kingdom, we must recognize that Jesus is speaking about the end times, about the close of this age, when the body of his followers will be united and all share together as one family. He is not talking primarily about payback in the here and now. And even at those times when Jesus may partially allude to economic reward in the here and now, he is not referring to some sort of voodoo economics or automatic blessing principles. Jesus is referring to the fact that even now his disciples take care of each other, just as Paul was later to say. Paul may allude to manna from heaven in 2 Corinthians 8–9, but he is not expecting aid to drop from the sky on the Jerusalem church. He is expecting his converts to do something about the problem by taking up a collection! The Corinthians are being asked to be the answer to the prayers of the Jerusalem church for aid.

It is something of an irony that the only time Paul really talks about money at length is when he is discussing the right of the minister to be paid, when he is discussing a special collection for the needy in a church that he didn't even plant, or when he is busy warning Timothy and others about becoming mercenaries rather than proper ministers. Never once does Paul talk about a weekly collection for the local congregation. He just assumes they know that since they are brothers and sisters in Christ, they take care of their own under the principle of "do good especially to the household of faith."

One of the significant lacunae in Blomberg's discussion of possessions and wealth is that he fails to really talk about systemic economic evil, for example in an economy based on slave labor. While Paul did not have a problem with patronage and reciprocity in some contexts, he did have a problem with slavery. He did not want any of his converts to become slaves. Slavery was seen by Paul as a violation of the principles of brotherhood and sisterhood in Christ. This is why he works so hard to persuade Philemon to accept Onesimus back "no longer as a slave, but rather as a brother in Christ."[8] Paul does indeed, where there is time and opportunity, strive for equality of personhood within the body of Christ. And as we have emphasized, this equality in Christ implies—at a minimum—assuring that there are no Christians in want or need. (James would have simply said Amen to this approach.) Paul's approach also means that "in house" the church should deconstruct the very basis of Rome's economy—slave labor.

John of Patmos provides much sterner warnings than Paul about the dangers of becoming enmeshed in a wicked economic system for the sake of becoming rich. He warns against getting in bed with wicked rulers for the sake of making money or a profit. He warns about the deadening effect of wealth on the human spirit and spiritual life. He knows how it is paradoxically easier for the poor person to get close to God and not make the mistake of seeing material things as that in which one should place one's trust. Like James (see James 5), John envisions a gloomy future for rich merchants who engage in predatory practices and shady business deals, and honor the false gods of this world rather than the one true God. No wonder Jesus said it is easier for a camel to crawl through the eye of a needle than for a rich person to enter God's kingdom!

In short, in light of the New Testament we need both a micro- and a macroethic when it comes to matters of money, wealth, possessions, work, remuneration, and the like. It is not enough simply to be an honest person earning an honest dollar. Our business ethics must match our Christian principles. If one has considerable assets one has to ask hard questions, such as, Has this money been made while investing in wicked enterprises and compromising companies? One must work to disentangle oneself from the ways of the world and its business-as-usual attitude and conventions.

There are, of course, other difficult issues to address, issues about which the New Testament is entirely silent. I am thinking, for example, about retirement. There is nothing in the Bible that either encourages or validates our consideration of retirement, unless we are already dying. The whole idea of saving up huge sums of money for oneself and one's family so one can live a life of ease or luxury, having no need to work any longer, is an all too modern notion without any biblical warrant.[9]

John Wesley prayed, "Lord, don't let me live to be idle," and he meant it. This does not lead to the conclusion that we should simply live to work, for there is a place for play and rest as well. Working to make a living is right and normal where one has the health to do so. But the connection between work, life, ministry, and Christian behavior requires more careful thought. If the purpose of making money now is so one can live in luxury and idleness later, that is *not* a Christian motivation. If the motive is so that one can be more involved in and support Christian causes and ministries later, that is another matter.

What is clear is that we must not silence the repeated New Testament warnings about the deleterious effects of wealth on one's spiritual life. The New Testament as a whole encourages us to have generous hearts. It encourages us not to live our lives working for "unrighteous mammon" in a self-seeking and self-centered manner. It encourages us to put our ultimate trust in God, and be willing to demonstrate that trust through sacrificial giving. It encourages us to be wary of and wise about the fallen economic and political institutions of this world, and to do our best to disengage from their unethical practices. The New Testament urges us to have a theology of enough, that is, to live by a principle that godliness with contentment leads to great gain in ways that can't be monetarily quantified. The New Testament encourages us to deconstruct and disengage from the rat race for success, prosperity, and wealth. Greed is repeatedly warned against as a soul-destroying force. The goal of the Christian life is not prosperity or even happiness but rather godliness and holiness, loving God and neighbor wholeheartedly.

Notice that the great commandment that Jesus reiterates is in essence a clarion call to come out of our self-centered, self-focused, self-indulgent lifestyles and love God and others with exuberance and abundance. When we do that, generosity becomes as natural as breathing, not an onerous task to which one has to be exhorted repeatedly. Of course the concern in the New Testament that we not become burdens to others when we can carry our own loads is notable. Idlers should not expect to eat at the expense of another's hard work. Within the body of Christ all are expected to work and be prepared when a crisis comes to help those in need. Work is not seen as a curse, but a blessing and an opportunity to gain resources so one can be a blessing to others.

The New Testament does not promise a quid pro quo return on financial investments in the body of Christ or—better said—it does not promise an equivalent monetary boon for whatever amount one gives to a good Christian purpose or ministry. One is to give with no thought of return. But there is also the promise that God does bless in various ways those who generously give to others. The exhortations in 2 Corinthians 8–9 need to be considered closely on this particular issue, for they remind us that Paul does not encourage calculation, by which I mean he does not encourage the Corinthians to assume that God will automatically give them back more than they have contributed to the collection for the Jerusalem church. Nothing in this or any other New Testament text suggests such a conclusion. When Jesus physically invested his life for us and made the full and final sacrifice on the cross, this resulted in spiritual benefits for us. Sometimes the rewards for material generosity are simply spiritual, and rightly seen those rewards are in fact more precious and valuable in the kingdom schema of things.

The New Testament repeatedly and insistently asks if we have counted the cost of discipleship, taking up our cross and following Jesus. In other words, the New Testament asks if we have embraced kingdom principles when it comes to money, possessions, wealth, ministry, remuneration, and work. If we have not done so, or have not done so sufficiently, then there is still something we can do about it. In our final chapter we will talk about how to deprogram oneself from a lifestyle that will kill one's spiritual life—the lifestyle of conspicuous consumption.

10

Deprogramming Ourselves from a Lifestyle of Conspicuous Consumption and Self-Gratification

If gold rusts, what then will iron do?

—Chaucer (comparing ministers
to laity on the matter of example
and moral character)

When it's a question of money, everybody is of the same religion.

—Voltaire

I was in seminary when an important and controversial book hit the bookstores—Ron Sider's still relevant *Rich Christians in an Age of Hunger*. I remember very clearly the varied reactions to this call for North American Christians to simplify their lives, de-enculturate themselves from the culture of constant consumption, and begin to devote themselves to meaningful ministry to the poor. It amazed me that the reactions to this book were sometimes not merely visceral or volatile, but almost violent. Sider hit a nerve, deep in the soul of evangelical Christianity, a very tender and raw nerve. He had spoken truth to power, and power did not like it. This book was followed by an equally important little gem of a treatise by Gordon Fee, *The Disease of the Health and Wealth Gospel*. In that book Fee forcefully deconstructed the prosperity gospel long before it ever became the stuff of modern best sellers and TV superstars. There was nothing left of the notion that "Jesus was rich, and he wants all ya'll to be rich" when this little treatise ended.

Yet, large segments of the church did not listen and did not want to listen, and it appears that is even more true today at the beginning of the twenty-first century than it was then. The saddest part about all this is that it involves a fundamental betrayal of Jesus's vision of what the in-breaking kingdom of God was supposed to be and look like. Jesus did not live a life of self-sacrifice and die on the cross in order to set up the First Church of Conspicuous Consumption and the Upwardly Mobile. Indeed, Jesus spoke of the least, the last, and the lost being first to enter the kingdom of God; and the first, the most, and the found being in danger of never entering it. So, how do we deprogram ourselves from the seductive values of our culture when it comes to materialism and conspicuous consumption? Let's start with an obvious point and move on from there.

1. Don't Even Go There!

What we don't give to a person who is drowning is more water. The same principle applies to a person awash in possessions (or lusting to be awash in possessions). There are of course passages in the New Testament that suggest or imply that it's fine to have possessions, though good stewardship is required. But when a text like "seek first the kingdom and all these things will be added unto you" gets ripped out of its context and the assumption is made that "all these things" are not merely necessities but include luxuries, then we do in fact violate the character of even the texts that imply it is not a sin to have possessions. More to the point, we violate the whole thrust of the New Testament, which is quite in the opposite direction.

The emphasis of the New Testament lies not on the acquisition side of things (using one's piety and prayer to get what one wants from the God who runs the ultimate Super Store) but on sacrifice and divestiture. Instead of a prosperity gospel, modern affluent Christians mostly need to hear the gospel of divestiture and self-sacrifice. In other words, when it comes to a biblical view of money and prosperity we don't start by encouraging a person to baptize the materialistic values of the larger culture and call them good.

2. Develop a Good Sense of the Difference between Necessities and Luxuries

Jesus encourages us to pray for daily bread, in effect for the necessities of life—food, shelter, clothing, family, friends, a means of working and living. Most everything beyond that is a luxury. I would encourage everyone to read carefully John Wesley's sermon in appendix 2 of this book as we begin to process this issue. It's true that one person's luxury is another person's necessity. It often depends on one's circumstances and setting. My wife and I did not need a refrigerator when we lived in Durham, England as the climate was quite clement and temperate. But I can't imagine living in Singapore without a refrigerator (or at least a shared one). If a person is a diabetic and his or her medicine must be refrigerated, then a refrigerator is a necessity. In other words, *discernment* and wisdom are necessary in order to determine what is a necessity and what a luxury for a particular person. Let's take another couple of examples.

I am a teacher, and I could not do my job without books. Indeed, I am a research professor and I write a lot of books, and this requires sources. Of course I can get many of them in or through a library, but not all. And some I cannot use for extended periods of time when they are on loan from another library. What should I do about this? Years ago I came to the conclusion that the smart move was to carefully build my own library, which I have done over the last twenty-five years. I intend someday to bequeath most of it to a theological library. In the meantime, I am very thankful that I have it and can use it continually. I have perhaps three thousand theological books. Have I overinvested in books? When was enough, enough? It can be hard to know. Thankfully, though, I am now at the point where I don't have to buy many books and I have started to divest.

When I started out my position was similar to that of a doctor who needs his or her diagnostic texts and reference books. And they are costly. I do know that I would not be the scholar I have become if I did not have this library. For one thing, it allowed me to do work anywhere. I could work at home when the kids were small. I could pack up my books and take them to Timbuktu when I was on sabbatical. I am now at the point where the scales have tipped in the direction towards my having to justify buying a book, rather than justify not buying it. But this is precisely the sort of discernment process I expect to go through as I try to simplify my life, and continue to wage the ongoing battle of de-enculturation from our society's dominant non-Christian values. It is not an easy struggle, but we are called to be in the world without being of it.

Paul enunciates the matter this way: from now on we should live "as if not" (1 Corinthians 7). What he means by this is that we should live with a sense of detachment from all the institutions and "forms" of this world. I quite agree with this. We live between the two advents of Christ, which means we are already in the eschatological age and should live on the basis of kingdom values, not the world's values. Sometimes, however, it becomes hard to tell the difference.

One thing I have learned to say is "never say never" when it comes to what God may ask of me. If Jesus asked his initial disciples to leave hearth, home, wife, and children behind and come follow him, it follows from this that he may require stringent sacrifices of any of us at some point in our lives. So when we are evaluating the differences between necessities and luxuries we need to pause before we say "God would never ask me to give or give up X."

There are some clear guidelines in the New Testament when it comes to obvious luxury that is to be avoided—expensive clothes, ridiculously expensive jewelry, unnecessarily large gas-guzzling luxury vehicles, enormous houses with rooms that are seldom if ever used, and we could go on. But these are easy targets for criticism. Should a Christian dentist spend a million dollars on the latest X-ray imaging equipment, or be satisfied with less high-tech fare? Chances are that he will not lose business just because he doesn't have the latest gadget, and the question to be asked is, Is it necessary to my work, or would it simply be nice to have?

My suggestion is that every Christian should begin to draw up a list of his or her own necessities of life, and then list the luxuries. This will require a good deal of thought, and the process alone is beneficial because it fosters critical thinking about one's lifestyle and whether or not it is godly. This process of discernment and de-enculturation is crucial to spiritual health, and for freeing ourselves to do more for the kingdom, with less focus on self and one's own family.

3. Make a Commitment to Ministerial Projects That Require a Sacrifice

There is such a stress on taking care of the poor and the indigent in the Bible that it seems clear that one priority for almost every Christian is involvement in the ministries of compassion. Such involvement can be financial support, mission trips, and indeed even relocating so one can engage in such ministries. Two of my students have deliberately moved to the very poorest part of Lexington, Kentucky to reach out to that community. Our whole church is backing them with all sorts of support and commitment. There is a side benefit to getting involved in a ministry of compassion. Once one travels to Kenya to dig a well for a village without water and goes to New Orleans to help the homeless, poverty takes on real faces and the poor are no longer "those people." Then it's hard to keep living the lifestyle of the rich and famous without a guilty conscience. Guilt in this case is good, if it reflects an awareness that we are living a self-centered rather than a God-centered life.

4. If Making Money Is No Longer an Issue, Devote the Rest of Your Life to Ministry Projects

Retirement in the normal secular sense of the term is not really a viable option for a committed Christian who remains healthy. But consider what two friends of mine did. They live in Woodlands, Texas. After many years of working for the oil industry, Bob, having saved up enough money, decided to invest himself in a variety of mission projects. His wife became an ordained minister and now serves her church well and wisely, having been freed up to do so through the wise use of the money already earned. If only there were more Christians like them, and less like those who drive around in gas-guzzling motor homes with bumper stickers bragging, "I'm spending my children's inheritance"!

5. Evaluate Your Budget, Especially Discretionary Spending Funds

This ought to be obvious, but some people are dumbfounded when they discover how much of their surplus money is simply being wasted instead of being put to good use. One of the real problems in living in a culture like ours is that there are so many stimuli urging us to spend that we can get to the point of feeling that we must do so, *even when we don't need the product at all.* I've met Christians who think it is their patriotic duty to buy American "stuff," even if it's pure junk and not even close to being a necessity of life. One thing we certainly should do to simplify our lifestyles is to make sure we are on the "no call" list for solicitors of various sorts. And another thing: don't make any financial commitments to such persons over the phone—ever!

6. Decrease the Amount of Waste in Your Life

Yes, I am talking about recycling all sorts of things. But in addition to that we need to evaluate how much food, clothing, and the like is simply being thrown away for no good reason. That should never happen. Waste not, want not. No more groaning about leftovers. Don't take more food than one can and should eat, and when eating out, if the portions are too large then share, or bring it home and eat it later. Period.

In these and other ways, it's a matter of Christian witness that we go green as rapidly as possible. This means hybrid cars, and smaller cars in general. It means energy-efficient light bulbs, and solar panels if possible. It means don't leave the air conditioning running if no one is home most of the day, and so on. Increasingly, we need to be conservers, not just consumers.

7. Hang Out with the Holy Rollers, Not the High Rollers

Psychologists are perfectly clear that people emulate and often become like those they admire. One of the ways to simplify our lives is to stop trying to keep up with the Joneses, or even hanging out with them. The simple but seductive influence of envy, which leads to imitation, is less powerful if we do not regularly hang out with people who are dripping in bling and up to their eyeballs in hock due to their oversized house, car, boat, and lifestyle. By contrast, when we start hanging out with people who have simplified their lifestyle, if we are not already that way then we may become helpfully self-critical. We begin to realize the need to change some things.

Stop trying to apply a consumer and competitive mentality to a Christian lifestyle. There are certain psychological dynamics that drive any culture, and two of the most obvious in our culture are the consumer and competitive drives. There are so many Christians who are consumer junkies or competition junkies. They have to go to the mall, play some type of game or watch a game, or they are just plain bored with life. This word just in: boredom is the state of mind of those who lack imagination, especially Christian imagination. Try to stop evaluating your church from a consumer point of view. Don't choose a church based on where *you can get the most out of it*, but on where you can best serve. What I am saying is that the consumer mentality is a form of the primal sin of self-focus, self-centeredness. And the competitive mentality, especially if not properly channeled, can destroy friendships and marriages. This kind of destructive competiveness ultimately goes back to Cain and Abel. It is sibling rivalry writ large.

For those who want a fight worth fighting, go fight the war on drugs, on sin, on pornography, on the sex trade, on sexual promiscuity and abortion. For those who want to compete, compete to be the best parent, spouse, or Sunday school teacher you can be. I am not saying that all competition is bad. There are of course athletic metaphors in the New Testament. The question is, What really constitutes winning? Have we won anything worth having if we've cheated to get it? Have we won anything worth having if it leads to the alienation of our fellow Christians? Christians have to be in the business of redefining success and winning, or placing it so far down on our priority list after compassion, love of neighbor, nurturing the community, and the like that it looks very different.

Let me give an example here. One of the persons I most admire in all of sports is Darrell Green, an all-pro defensive player for the Redskins for many years, who led by example. His faith in Christ was the most important thing in his life, and winning football games was entirely secondary. But as a Christian he committed himself to excellence, to striving for perfection, to doing and being all he could do and be to set a good example for his teammates. He was an absolute team player. When the Lord told him to stay in Washington, even when he had multiple, more lucrative opportunities to go elsewhere, he stayed. He had a church and a family that meant everything to him, and they were of higher priority than making more money in his life.

Green stayed in Washington through the ups and downs of Redskin history, and in 2008 he was inducted into the Hall of Fame. What was especially striking to me was that he was inducted not by his coach, but by his son. And what his son kept saying about him is that he had been a great role model of a godly father and he wanted to be like his father. Here is an example of how Christian values can trump cultural values, without compromising one's integrity and without failing to promote one's best in one's profession. This is indeed being in the world, and providing a good witness to it, without being of the world. A Christian needs not only to have his or her priorities straight, when it comes to what is really valuable in life, but also to know what the nonnegotiables are. It's no use gaining the whole world and losing one's soul.

8. Stop Assuming That There Are No Problems with Capitalism

The Bible doesn't present us with either communistic or capitalistic options when it comes to the economy. There is a theological reason as well as a historical one for this. The theory of property in the Bible is that God is the owner of all things. When it comes to the Bible's viewpoint, neither the government nor private individuals really own anything. Rather, we are all just stewards of God's property, and God can do what God likes with it. The question is, Are we in tune with God's preferences about such matters?

If the philosophy of capitalism is "what's mine is mine, and if I choose to share it, I am philanthropic" and the philosophy of communism is "what's yours is actually ours and we must confiscate it or treat it as public property," then neither of these philosophical approaches to property will do from a Christian point of view. Christians need to constantly be assessing what good stewardship of the personal property we have from God looks like. We need to regularly ask: God, what would you have me do with this? Why have you given it to me? Too often the assumption of the health and wealth preachers is that one is simply in the "bless me" club and that is the end of the discussion. But in fact, as Paul so aptly reminds us, we are blessed in order to be a blessing to others, which is precisely why we must keep asking why this or that has been given to us. Gratitude is not enough as a response to grace. Responsibility and inquiry as to the purpose and function of a gift is in order.

We must be honest that there are some severe problems with capitalism (even free market capitalism) from a Christian point of view. Capitalism tends towards an endless focus on making money and buying new things to keep the economy growing. It has led to the lust for ever-cheaper goods, even at the expense of home-grown mom and pop companies that are forced out of business because most everything has to be outsourced so we can enjoy low prices. I must confess, though, that I have mixed feelings about this, because we now have a global economy, and I have no problems with other countries improving the lot in life of their people through my purchases. But in the twenty-first century we must be global Christians, not just global capitalists. That means we must care about the well-being of the world in general, and Christians worldwide in particular.

Having said this, it is clear enough to me that capitalism is probably the lesser of two evils if the alternative is communism, especially Marxist communism. I have spent enough time teaching in formerly communist countries to see that it did not benefit the people in any appreciable way. Indeed, it kept most of them in poverty. And the issue is not just democracy versus communism. I am clear that the former as a political system is more biblical than the latter, especially when it comes to religious freedom. But the larger issue is the Marxist economic system of absolute state control. I find it difficult to understand why so many biblical scholars think that Marxist analysis, process, and economic theory are more in accord with the New Testament than other theories. Indeed, it seems to me that the John of Patmos who critiqued Rome and its slave-based totalitarian economy would have a similar reaction to anti-Christian Marxist governments and their totalitarian, centrally-organized economies.

Learn to listen to others who are older and wiser, those who have spent considerable time simplifying their own lifestyles. The Wisdom literature of the Bible tells us that it is helpful to go to those who have reflected long and carefully about how to live a genuinely biblical life. The Old Testament speaks of how we should wish for neither wealth nor poverty, the New Testament about how godliness with contentment and a theology of enough should govern our lifestyle.

Wisdom does not assume that we are not spiritually affected by what we own, by how we regard our possessions. It is not biblical wisdom to assume that God wants us all to be wealthy. Frankly, most fallen persons, and even most Christian persons, can't handle wealth properly. It goes to their heads, to their hearts, not to mention to their stomachs. They give way to the delusion that they are special and thus better than the *hoi polloi* of society, or, even worse, they become convinced that they must be truly godly or God would not have blessed them with all this stuff. Wealth all too easily leads to delusion.

Nor does wisdom assume that "things," and especially a surfeit of things, don't get in the way of our relationship with God. The Bible actually suggests that things pose the danger of becoming our god when our acquisitive instinct runs on overdrive. I personally have learned a great deal from Christians who have successfully resisted the consumer mentality, choosing instead to follow the path of a simple lifestyle.

My grandfather and grandmother were always on that track, and it wasn't solely because they lived through the Great Depression. It was because they were profoundly committed Christians, dedicated to serving others even when they had little. My mother has told me how they gave $6 a week to the poor and indigent at a time when my grandfather only made $20 a week at the fire department. But that was not all. My grandfather lived this life in the shadow of the afterlife. Once I asked him, "Grandfather, why are you such a straight arrow?" His answer was unforgettable: "Heaven is too sweet and hell is too hot to mess around in this life." My grandfather was like those first Christians. He did not allow his culture to determine his approach to money, wealth, work, remuneration, and the like. He knew that this world was not intended to be the be all and end all of life, and so he lived this life in the shadow of eternity, at the doorstep of the kingdom. He sat lightly with possessions, and never felt compelled to shop until he dropped. He gave sacrificially not only to his church but to many others as well. And he died at ninety-two years of age a happy and holy man, a loved and successful man according to the standards of the Bible.

9. Declare a Jubilee Year, Forgiving Someone Who Owes You a Debt and Lending Money Interest Free

In our discussion of the ministry of Jesus we pointed out that he announced the coming of the kingdom by proclaiming a year of Jubilee (Luke 4). We can see further evidence of this not only in Jesus's general discussion about forgiveness but probably in the Lord's Prayer itself. There the disciple is tutored in prayer to ask for forgiveness of debts, and this is linked to forgiving those who are indebted to oneself. Obviously there are times and places where it is a good thing to let persons work their way out of debt, especially if they have acted irresponsibly. But there is also a time to forgive debts as well, especially when debtors have worked hard and circumstances have conspired against them even though they have made a good-faith effort to pay off their debts. This applies at the national level as well. The West needs to get on with simply forgiving Third World debt.

The other side of this equation is about loaning money, and we have seen very clearly how various biblical writers were adamantly opposed to lending money at interest, *especially when it was one believer loaning money to another*. It is thus in order to suggest that one way to become a good witness and a better person is to ignore the old Shakespearean advice in act one of Hamlet, which some have mistakenly taken as a quote from the Bible:

> Neither a borrower nor a lender be;
> For loan oft loses both itself and friend,
> And borrowing dulls the edge of husbandry.
> This above all: to thine own self be true.

On the contrary, we should look for opportunities to help others and make sacrifices on their behalf. Lending money is one way to do this, and forgiving a debt is another way to practice generosity in the body of Christ. As we have seen, the Bible is all about giving with no thought of return. And if it is giving, it isn't merely lending, is it?

Tear up those credit cards! America has become a nation that binges on credit, especially high-interest credit cards. One way to really help simplify one's own life and lifestyle is to pay all bills on time and in full, using either cash or perhaps a debit card. It's okay to have one credit card reserved for emergencies, but if we keep a careful budget, there should be few occasions that demand its use.

Consider this list simply as a starter kit. The goal here is to cultivate the same giving and generous spirit we see in Jesus and various of his earliest followers. The emphasis on giving *with no thought of return* is and should be seen as a challenge to reciprocity conventions and the whole payback mentality. Jesus even urged giving *to one's enemies* with no thought of return. (This reminds me of a bumper sticker I saw recently: "Love your enemies. It will confuse them.")

Jesus and the New Testament call us to a countercultural, and in some cases a counterintuitive, kingdom ethic when it comes to money, wealth, sacrificial giving, work, and remuneration. Instead of baptizing his own culture's basic assumptions about money and wealth, Jesus constantly challenged those assumptions, and we should do likewise.

Ten Christian Myths about Money

Myth One: If you just trust God, he will give you "all the desires of your heart."

What the Scripture in question actually says is, "Delight yourself in the LORD, and He shall give you the desires of your heart. Commit your way to the LORD, trust also in Him, and He shall bring it to pass" (Ps. 37:4, 5). This saying has nothing necessarily to do with economic prosperity. The desire of the heart referred to here is God. If you delight in God he will bless you with more of the divine presence is all the psalmist has in view.

Myth Two: If you "seek first the kingdom," then God will give you all the things you long for.

Again, this is a profound misreading of what the biblical text says. Jesus in Matthew 6:25–34 has been talking about the basic necessities in life—food, clothing, and the like. He tells his disciples they should not be anxious even about the necessities in life, not least because God knows we need such things to survive. Instead of anxious worrying we are to seek first the kingdom, and then these necessities will be added to us. In this context Jesus says nothing about blessing us with wealth or anything like it. He refers only to basic food, drink, and clothing.

Myth Three: If you tithe, then God will necessarily bless you far more than you have given. This is based on sayings like: "Ask and it will be given to you" (Matt. 7:7).

Again the context here is that of asking for a basic necessity—mere bread or a fish to eat! Jesus reassures us that when we seek such things from God, he is able to provide. This does indicate that God enjoys blessing those who seek him and his aid in these matters. It suggests that God has an infinite store of such things, one that never runs out. So there is some truth to the saying "you have not because you ask not" when it comes to basic necessities. But texts like this say nothing about a quid pro quo, or a reciprocity cycle with God. Often the blessings of God are not material ones in any case. And the notion that we can put God in our debt, so that he is bound by promissory note to give us Y because we gave him X is simply false. God's gifts are free and gracious, not things owed to someone operating out of a misguided theology of reciprocity.

Myth Four: If we are just sincere enough in our asking, or simply pray long and fervently enough, God is bound to give us what we ask for.

This whole approach seems to view prayer as a means of strong-arming a God who is reluctant to help. This notion is entirely false on both sides of the equation. First of all, we can't make God an offer he can't refuse, no matter how nicely or insistently we ask. Why not? Because all too often what we ask for is not at all what we need or what will benefit our Christian growth. Second, God is obligated only to do what he has already promised to do, and even then it will depend on whether or not the thing in question was part of a conditional promise. When God begins a promise along the lines of "if my people who are called by my name will repent and turn to me, then . . . ," we need to understand that if we don't fulfill our half of the conditional statement God is under no obligation to fulfill his half.

Myth Five: Money is the root of all evil, hence the nicknames "filthy lucre" or "unrighteous mammon." Therefore, it's better for Christians simply not to focus on making money, which is at best a necessary evil.

What Paul actually says is that the *love of money* is a root of all sorts of evil. In other words, it is the attitude of one's heart towards money that is being critiqued, which includes the sin called greed. Money in itself is just a means of exchange. It is no more inherently evil than any other material thing God created. The warnings in the Bible, however, remind us that fallen human beings find things like money a great temptation to various and detrimental indulgences. This is why Jesus called such resources "unrighteous mammon." This being the case, a very cautious approach to money is in order; we need to be reflective about how and why we think we need more money or wish to purchase this or that thing.

Myth Six: Lending money at interest is not a problem for those who see the Bible as the Word of God.

There are in fact numerous strictures in the Old Testament that speak to the issue of believers lending money or resources to other believers and charging interest. What the Bible does not say is that it is wrong to charge interest to nonbelievers. But the general tenor of the Old Testament teachings on this subject suggest that if someone is a member of one's community, even if they are "a stranger in the land," charging interest is probably disallowed, or at least discouraged. We can also turn this around and ask about the ethics of speculation and trying to procure huge rates of interest or return on one's money. Is it right for a Christian to play the stock market, buying low and selling high? The Bible says nothing directly about this. There were no stock markets in ancient economies. But the overall impression one gets is that whatever severs the connection between work and reward, between an honest day's pay for an honest day's work, is not a good thing. Speculation is too often an attempt to reap enormous rewards with very little effort or investment of time, money, and skill. This seems to run counter to the ethic of work found in various parts of the Bible.[1]

Myth Seven: As the examples of Solomon and others in the Old Testament show, God has no problems with a Christian being wealthy

In the first place, Christians are not under the old covenant, and the New Testament has a much stricter and higher standard for what counts as a godly life when it comes to material things. In the second place, even in Proverbs and elsewhere in the Old Testament critiques of kings like Solomon, who ape the emperors and kings of the ancient Near East with respect to wealth and opulence, indicate that this is not a good thing.

Myth Eight: As long as I am thankful and know where my blessings come from, maintaining an attitude of gratitude towards God, I can do whatever I please with my money, within certain obvious ethical bounds (e.g., not squandering it on sexually immoral practices).

This is profoundly false. The resources we have are indeed blessings from God, thus it is all the more necessary and expected that we treat them as God's resources and ask the question, What would please God in the disposition of the resources I have been given? This is why James and others accused Christians of stealing from the poor, the widow, and the orphan when they engage in conspicuous consumption or an opulent lifestyle.

Myth Nine: Since we are saved by grace through faith, God will not hold us responsible for what we do with our money.

This is false, and but a variant of the notion that since salvation is by grace, there is no accountability for deeds of any kind done after conversion. This way of thinking is a direct contradiction of texts like 2 Corinthians 5, which remind us that we must all appear before the judgment seat of Christ to give an account of the deeds we have done in the body. This is even more clear in the parable of the sheep and the goats, where Jesus berates his own disciples for not visiting him in prison, feeding him, and the like, and then says, "inasmuch as you have not done it to the least of these, you haven't done it to me." Jesus identifies with the plight of the poor and needy, and expects us to do the same.

Myth Ten: As a tithing Christian, I am free to do as I like with the 90 percent I have not tithed.

In the first place, the standard is sacrificial giving, which may mean more than a tithe in some cases. In the second place, the 90 percent still belongs to God. We are only its stewards and must use it in accordance with God's will.

In the end, it would be wise for us to take to heart and put into practice what Paul says about a theology of "enough," of godliness with contentment, which he calls "great gain." Philippians 4:11–13 is an excellent guide for the Christian life in this sort of matter. Can we as twenty-first-century Christians learn to be content, whatever our material circumstances? Or will we succumb to the siren song of advertisements that suggest to us all sorts of things we have to have, when in fact they are not necessities of life at all? Can we learn the secret of being content whether in plenty or in want? Paul says he learned to be content as a Christian in times of plenty as well as times of want. My prayer is that we too would learn this secret of contentment.

Appendix **2**

"The Use of Money"

A Sermon by John Wesley

What follows here is perhaps the most famous sermon ever preached on Christians and the use of money in the eighteenth century. It is the sermon that John Wesley preached more often than any other (save for his famous "Justification by Faith" sermon), especially late in the eighteenth century, when Methodists through their industry and frugality had begun in many cases to become prosperous. Wesley inherited Puritan ideas about money through his mother and through Puritan writings. But he placed his own stamp on the material, especially in his insistence on the third major point of his sermon—"give all you can"—which goes well beyond an appeal to tithe.

Wesley, it can be said, had the courage of his convictions. He gave away almost everything he had before he died. He lived frugally throughout his life so that resources could be freed up for all sorts of ministry causes, ranging from building orphanages to sending missionaries to America. In my view, this sermon is as needed and relevant for the church in North America today as it ever was. I am

172

providing here the older Jackson edition (1872) of the sermon, which has all the original Latin quotes, and is in the public domain.

The Use Of Money

"I say unto you, Make unto yourselves friends of the mammon of unrighteousness; that, when ye fail, they may receive you into the everlasting habitations." (Luke 16:9)

1. Our Lord, having finished the beautiful parable of the Prodigal Son, which he had particularly addressed to those who murmured at his receiving publicans and sinners, adds another relation of a different kind, addressed rather to the children of God. "He said unto his disciples"—not so much to the scribes and Pharisees to whom he had been speaking before—"There was a certain rich man, who had a steward, and he was accused to him of wasting his goods. And calling him, he said, 'Give an account of thy stewardship, for thou canst be no longer steward'" (Luke 16:1, 2). After reciting the method which the bad steward used to provide against the day of necessity, our Saviour adds, "His lord commended the unjust steward"—namely, in this respect, that he used timely precaution—and subjoins this weighty reflection, "The children of this world are wiser in their generation than the children of light" (Luke 16:8). Those who seek no other portion than this world "are wiser" (not absolutely, for they are one and all the veriest fools, the most egregious madmen under heaven, but, "in their generation," in their own way; they are more consistent with themselves; they are truer to their acknowledged principles; they more steadily pursue their end) "than the children of light"— than they who see "the light of the glory of God in the face of Jesus Christ." Then follow the words above recited: "And I"—the only-begotten Son of God, the Creator, Lord, and Possessor of heaven and earth and all that is therein; the Judge of all, to whom ye are to "give an account of your stewardship," when ye "can be no longer stewards"—"I say unto you,"—learn in this respect, even of the unjust steward,—"Make yourselves friends," by wise, timely precaution, "of the mammon of unrighteousness." "Mammon" means riches or money. It is termed "the mammon of unrighteousness," because of the unrighteous manner wherein it [is] frequently procured, and wherein even that which was honestly procured is generally employed. "Make yourselves friends" of this, by doing all possible good, particularly to the children of God; "that, when ye fail"—when ye return to dust,

when ye have no more place under the sun—those of them who are gone before "may receive you," may welcome you, into the "everlasting habitations."

2. An excellent branch of Christian wisdom is here inculcated by our Lord on all his followers, namely, the right use of money—a subject largely spoken of, after their manner, by men of the world; but not sufficiently considered by those whom God hath chosen out of the world. These, generally, do not consider, as the importance of the subject requires, the use of this excellent talent. Neither do they understand how to employ it to the greatest advantage; the introduction of which into the world is one admirable instance of the wise and gracious providence of God. It has, indeed, been the manner of poets, orators, and philosophers, in almost all ages and nations, to rail at this, as the grand corrupter of the world, the bane of virtue, the pest of human society. Hence nothing so commonly heard as:

> *Nocens ferrum, ferroque nocentius aurum:*
> And gold, more mischievous than keenest steel.

Hence the lamentable complaint,

> *Effodiuntur opes, irritamenta malorum.*
> Wealth is dug up, incentive to all ill.

Nay, one celebrated writer gravely exhorts his countrymen, in order to banish all vice at once, to " throw all their money into the sea":

> *. . . in mare proximum [. . .]*
> *Summi materiem mali!*

But is not all this mere empty rant? Is there any solid reason therein? By no means. For, let the world be as corrupt as it will, is gold or silver to blame? "The love of money," we know, "is the root of all evil"; but not the thing itself. The fault does not lie in the money, but in them that use it. It may be used ill: and what may not? But it may likewise be used well: It is full as applicable to the best, as to the worst uses. It is of unspeakable service to all civilized nations, in all the common affairs of life: It is a most compendious instrument of transacting all manner of business, and (if we use it according to Christian wisdom) of doing all manner of good. It is true, were man in a state of innocence, or were all men "filled with the Holy Ghost," so that, like the infant Church at Jerusalem, "no man counted anything he had his own," but "distribution was made to everyone as he had need," the use of it would be superseded; as we cannot conceive there is anything of the kind among the inhabitants of heaven. But, in the present state of mankind, it is an excellent gift of God, answering the noblest ends. In the hands of his children, it is food for the hungry, drink for the thirsty, raiment for the naked: It gives to the traveller and the stranger where to lay his head. By it we may supply the place of an husband to the widow, and of a father to the fatherless. We may be a defence for the oppressed, a means of health to the sick, of ease to them that are in pain; it may be as eyes to the blind, as feet to the lame; yea, a lifter up from the gates of death!

3. It is therefore of the highest concern that all who fear God know how to employ this valuable talent; that they be instructed how it may answer these glorious ends, and in the highest degree. And, perhaps, all the instructions which are necessary for this may be reduced to three plain rules, by the exact observance whereof we may approve ourselves faithful stewards of "the mammon of unrighteousness."

I.

1. The first of these is (he that heareth, let him understand!) "Gain all you can." Here we may speak like the children of the world: We meet them on their own ground. And it is our bounden duty to do this: We ought to gain all we can gain, without buying gold too dear, without paying more for it than it is worth. But this it is certain we ought not to do; we ought not to gain money at the expense of life, nor (which is in effect the same thing) at the expense of our health. Therefore, no gain whatsoever should induce us to enter into, or to continue in, any employ, which is of such a kind, or is attended with so hard or so long labour, as to impair our constitution. Neither should we begin or continue in any business which necessarily deprives us of proper seasons for food and sleep, in such a proportion as our nature requires. Indeed, there is a great difference here. Some employments are absolutely and totally unhealthy; as those which imply the dealing much with arsenic, or other equally hurtful minerals, or the breathing an air tainted with steams of melting lead, which must at length destroy the firmest constitution. Others may not be absolutely

unhealthy, but only to persons of a weak constitution. Such are those which require many hours to be spent in writing; especially if a person write sitting, and lean upon his stomach, or remain long in an uneasy posture. But whatever it is which reason or experience shows to be destructive of health or strength, that we may not submit to; seeing "the life is more" valuable "than meat, and the body than raiment." And if we are already engaged in such an employ, we should exchange it as soon as possible for some which, if it lessen our gain, will, however, not lessen our health.

2. We are, Secondly, to gain all we can without hurting our mind any more than our body. For neither may we hurt this. We must preserve, at all events, the spirit of an healthful mind. Therefore we may not engage or continue in any sinful trade, any that is contrary to the law of God, or of our country. Such are all that necessarily imply our robbing or defrauding the king of his lawful customs. For it is at least as sinful to defraud the king of his right, as to rob our fellow subjects. And the king has full as much right to his customs as we have to our houses and apparel. Other businesses there are, which however innocent in themselves, cannot be followed with innocence now at least, not in England; such, for instance, as will not afford a competent maintenance without cheating or lying, or conformity to some custom which [is] not consistent with a good conscience: These, likewise, are sacredly to be avoided, whatever gain they may be attended with provided we follow the custom of the trade; for to gain money we must not lose our souls. There are yet others which many pursue with perfect innocence, without hurting either their body or mind. And yet perhaps you cannot: Either they may entangle you in that company which would destroy your soul, and by repeated experiments it may appear that you cannot separate the one from the other, or there may be an idiosyncrasy—a peculiarity in your constitution of soul (as there is in the bodily constitution of many) by reason whereof that employment is deadly to you, which another may safely follow. So I am convinced, from many experiments, I could not study, to any degree of perfection, either mathematics, arithmetic, or algebra, without being a Deist, if not an Atheist: And yet others may study them all their lives without sustaining any inconvenience. None therefore can here determine for another; but every man must judge for himself, and abstain from whatever he in particular finds to be hurtful to his soul.

3. We are, Thirdly, to gain all we can without hurting our neighbour. But this we may not, cannot do, if we love our neighbour as ourselves. We cannot, if we love everyone as ourselves, hurt anyone *in his substance*. We cannot devour the increase of his lands, and perhaps the lands and houses themselves, by gaming, by overgrown bills (whether on account of physic, or law, or anything else), or by requiring or taking such interest as even the laws of our country forbid. Hereby all pawn-broking is excluded: Seeing, whatever good we might do thereby, all unprejudiced men see with grief to be abundantly overbalanced by the evil. And if it were otherwise, yet we are not allowed to "do evil that good may come." We cannot, consistent with brotherly love, sell our goods below the market price; we cannot study to ruin our neighbour's trade, in order to advance our own; much less can we entice away or receive any of his servants or workmen whom he has need of. None can gain by swallowing up his neighbour's substance, without gaining the damnation of hell!

4. Neither may we gain by hurting our neighbour *in his body*. Therefore we may not sell anything which tends to impair health. Such is, eminently, all that liquid fire, commonly called drams or spirituous liquors. It is true, these may have a place in medicine; they may be of use in some bodily disorders; although there would rarely be occasion for them were it not for the unskillfulness of the practitioner. Therefore, such as prepare and sell them *only for this end* may keep their conscience clear. But who are they? Who prepare and sell them only for this end? Do you know ten such distillers in England? Then excuse these. But all who sell them in the common way, to any that will buy, are poisoners general. They murder His Majesty's subjects by wholesale, neither does their eye pity or spare. They drive them to hell like sheep. And what is their gain? Is it not the blood of these men? Who then would envy their large estates and sumptuous palaces? A curse is in the midst of them: The curse of God cleaves to the stones, the timber, the furniture of them. The curse of God is in their gardens, their walks, their groves; a fire that burns to the nethermost hell! Blood, blood is there: The foundation, the floor, the walls, the roof are stained with blood! And canst thou hope, O thou man of blood, though thou art "clothed in scarlet and fine linen, and farest sumptuously every day"; canst thou hope to deliver down thy *fields of blood* to the third generation? Not so; for there is a God in heaven: Therefore, thy name shall soon be rooted

out. Like as those whom thou hast destroyed, body and soul, "thy memorial shall perish with thee!"

5. And are not they partakers of the same guilt, though in a lower degree, whether Surgeons, Apothecaries, or Physicians, who play with the lives or health of men, to enlarge their own gain? Who purposely lengthen the pain or disease which they are able to remove speedily? Who protract the cure of their patient's body in order to plunder his substance? Can any man be clear before God who does not shorten every disorder "as much as he can," and remove all sickness and pain "as soon as he can"? He cannot: For nothing can be more clear than that he does not "love his neighbour as himself"; than that he does not "do unto others as he would they should do unto himself."

6. This is dear-bought gain. And so is whatever is procured by hurting our neighbour *in his soul*; by ministering, suppose, either directly or indirectly, to his unchastity, or intemperance, which certainly none can do, who has any fear of God, or any real desire of pleasing Him. It nearly concerns all those to consider this, who have anything to do with taverns, victualling-houses, opera-houses, play-houses, or any other places of public, fashionable diversion. If these profit the souls of men, you are clear; your employment is good, and your gain innocent; but if they are either sinful in themselves, or natural inlets to sin of various kinds, then, it is to be feared, you have a sad account to make. O beware, lest God say in that day, "These have perished in their iniquity, but their blood do I require at thy hands!"

7. These cautions and restrictions being observed, it is the bounden duty of all who are engaged in worldly business to observe that first and great rule of Christian wisdom with respect to money, "Gain all you can." Gain all you can by honest industry. Use all possible diligence in your calling. Lose no time. If you understand yourself and your relation to God and man, you know you have none to spare. If you understand your particular calling as you ought, you will have no time that hangs upon your hands. Every business will afford some employment sufficient for every day and every hour. That wherein you are placed, if you follow it in earnest, will leave you no leisure for silly, unprofitable diversions. You have always something better to do, something that will profit you, more or less. And "whatsoever thy hand findeth to do, do it with thy might." Do it as soon as possible: No delay! No putting off from day to day, or from hour to hour! Never leave anything till to-morrow, which you can do to-day. And do it as well as possible. Do not sleep or yawn over it: Put your whole

strength to the work. Spare no pains. Let nothing be done by halves, or in a slight and careless manner. Let nothing in your business be left undone if it can be done by labour or patience.

8. Gain all you can, by common sense, by using in your business all the understanding which God has given you. It is amazing to observe how few do this; how men run on in the same dull track with their forefathers. But whatever they do who know not God, this is no rule for you. It is a shame for a Christian not to improve upon *them*, in whatever he takes in hand. You should be continually learning, from the experience of others, or from your own experience, reading, and reflection, to do everything you have to do better to-day than you did yesterday. And see that you practise whatever you learn, that you may make the best of all that is in your hands.

II.

1. Having gained all you can, by honest wisdom and unwearied diligence, the second rule of Christian prudence is, "Save all you can." Do not throw the precious talent into the sea: Leave that folly to heathen philosophers. Do not throw it away in idle expenses, which is just the same as throwing it into the sea. Expend no part of it merely to gratify the desire of the flesh, the desire of the eye, or the pride of life.

2. Do not waste any part of so precious a talent merely in gratifying the desires of the flesh; in procuring the pleasures of sense of whatever kind; particularly, in enlarging the pleasure of tasting. I do not mean, avoid gluttony and drunkenness only: An honest heathen would condemn these. But there is a regular, reputable kind of sensuality, an elegant epicurism, which does not immediately disorder the stomach, nor (sensibly, at least) impair the understanding. And yet (to mention no other effects of it now) it cannot be maintained without considerable expense. Cut off all this expense! Despise delicacy and variety, and be content with what plain nature requires.

3. Do not waste any part of so precious a talent merely in gratifying the desire of the eye by superfluous or expensive apparel, or by needless ornaments. Waste no part of it in curiously adorning your houses; in superfluous or expensive furniture; in costly pictures, painting, gilding, books; in elegant rather than useful gardens. Let your neighbours, who know nothing better, do this: "Let the dead bury

their dead." But "what is that to thee?" says our Lord: "Follow thou me." Are you willing? Then you are able so to do.

4. Lay out nothing to gratify the pride of life, to gain the admiration or praise of men. This motive of expense is frequently interwoven with one or both of the former. Men are expensive in diet, or apparel, or furniture, not barely to please their appetite, or to gratify their eye, their imagination, but their vanity too. "So long as thou dost well unto thyself, men will speak good of thee." So long as thou art "clothed in purple and fine linen, and farest sumptuously every day," no doubt many will applaud thy elegance of taste, thy generosity and hospitality. But do not buy their applause so dear. Rather be content with the honour that cometh from God.

5. Who would expend anything in gratifying these desires if he considered that to gratify them is to increase them? Nothing can be more certain than this: Daily experience shows, the more they are indulged, they increase the more. Whenever, therefore, you expend anything to please your taste or other senses, you pay so much for sensuality. When you lay out money to please your eye, you give so much for an increase of curiosity—for a stronger attachment to these pleasures which perish in the using. While you are purchasing anything which men use to applaud, you are purchasing more vanity. Had you not then enough of vanity, sensuality, curiosity before? Was there need of any addition? And would you pay for it, too? What manner of wisdom is this? Would not the literally throwing your money into the sea be a less mischievous folly?

6. And why should you throw away money upon your children, any more than upon yourself, in delicate food, in gay or costly apparel, in superfluities of any kind? Why should you purchase for them more pride or lust, more vanity, or foolish and hurtful desires? They do not want any more; they have enough already; nature has made ample provision for them: Why should you be at farther expense to increase their temptations and snares, and to pierce them through with more sorrows?

7. Do not leave it to them to throw away. If you have good reason to believe that they would waste what is now in your possession in gratifying and thereby increasing the desire of the flesh, the desire of the eye, or the pride of life at the peril of theirs and your own soul, do not set these traps in their way. Do not offer your sons or your daughters unto Belial, any more than unto Moloch. Have pity upon them, and remove out of their way what you may easily foresee

would increase their sins, and consequently plunge them deeper into everlasting perdition! How amazing then is the infatuation of those parents who think they can never leave their children enough! What! Cannot you leave them enough of arrows, firebrands, and death? Not enough of foolish and hurtful desires? Not enough of pride, lust, ambition, vanity? Not enough of everlasting burnings? Poor wretch! Thou fearest where no fear is. Surely both thou and they, when ye are lifting up your eyes in hell, will have enough both of the "worm that never dieth," and of "the fire that never shall be quenched"!

8. "What then would you do, if you was in my case? If you had a considerable fortune to leave?" Whether I *would* do it or no, I know what I *ought* to do: This will admit of no reasonable question. If I had one child, elder or younger, who knew the value of money; one who I believed, would put it to the true use, I should think it my absolute, indispensable duty to leave that child the bulk of my fortune; and to the rest just so much as would enable them to live in the manner they had been accustomed to do. "But what if all your children were equally ignorant of the true use of money?" I ought then (hard saying! Who can hear it?) to give each what would keep him above want, and to bestow all the rest in such a manner as I judged would be most for the glory of God.

III.

1. But let not any man imagine that he has done anything, barely by going thus far, by "gaining and saving all he can," if he were to stop here. All this is nothing, if a man go not forward, if he does not point all this at a farther end. Nor, indeed, can a man properly be said to save anything, if he only lays it up. You may as well throw your money into the sea, as bury it in the earth. And you may as well bury it in the earth, as in your chest, or in the Bank of England. Not to use, is effectually to throw it away. If, therefore, you would indeed "make yourselves friends of the mammon of unrighteousness," add the Third rule to the two preceding. Having, First, gained all you can, and, Secondly, saved all you can, Then "give all you can."

2. In order to see the ground and reason of this, consider, when the Possessor of heaven and earth brought you into being, and placed you in this world, he placed you here not as a proprietor, but a steward: As such he entrusted you, for a season, with goods of various kinds;

but the sole property of these still rests in him, nor can be alienated from him. As you yourself are not your own, but his, such is, likewise, all that you enjoy. Such is your soul and your body, not your own, but God's. And so is your substance in particular. And he has told you, in the most clear and express terms, how you are to employ it for him, in such a manner, that it may be all an holy sacrifice, acceptable through Christ Jesus. And this light, easy service, he has promised to reward with an eternal weight of glory.

3. The directions which God has given us, touching the use of our worldly substance, may be comprised in the following particulars. If you desire to be a faithful and a wise steward, out of that portion of your Lord's goods which he has for the present lodged in your hands, but with the right of resuming whenever it pleases him, First, provide things needful for yourself: food to eat, raiment to put on, whatever nature moderately requires for preserving the body in health and strength. Secondly, provide these for your wife, your children, your servants, or any others who pertain to your household. If when this is done there be an overplus left, then "do good to them that are of the household of faith." If there be an overplus still, "as you have opportunity, do good unto all men." In so doing, you give all you can; nay, in a sound sense, all you have: For all that is laid out in this manner is really given to God. You "render unto God the things that are God's," not only by what you give to the poor, but also by that which you expend in providing things needful for yourself and your household.

4. If, then, a doubt should at any time arise in your mind concerning what you are going to expend, either on yourself or any part of your family, you have an easy way to remove it. Calmly and seriously inquire, "(1) In expending this, am I acting according to my character? Am I acting herein, not as a proprietor, but as a steward of my Lord's goods? (2) Am I doing this in obedience to his Word? In what Scripture does he require me so to do? (3) Can I offer up this action, this expense, as a sacrifice to God through Jesus Christ? (4) Have I reason to believe that for this very work I shall have a reward at the resurrection of the just?" You will seldom need anything more to remove any doubt which arises on this head; but by this four-fold consideration you will receive clear light as to the way wherein you should go.

5. If any doubt still remain, you may farther examine yourself by prayer according to those heads of inquiry. Try whether you can say to

the Searcher of hearts, your conscience not condemning you, "Lord, thou seest I am going to expend this sum on that food, apparel, furniture. And thou knowest, I act herein with a single eye as a steward of thy goods, expending this portion of them thus in pursuance of the design thou hadst in entrusting me with them. Thou knowest I do this in obedience to the Lord, as thou commandest, and because thou commandest it. Let this, I beseech thee, be an holy sacrifice, acceptable through Jesus Christ! And give me a witness in myself that for this labour of love I shall have a recompense when thou rewardest every man according to his works." Now if your conscience bear you witness in the Holy Ghost that this prayer is well-pleasing to God, then have you no reason to doubt but that expense is right and good, and such as will never make you ashamed.

6. You see then what it is to "make yourselves friends of the mammon of unrighteousness," and by what means you may procure, "that when ye fail they may receive you into the everlasting habitations." You see the nature and extent of truly Christian prudence so far as it relates to the use of that great talent, money. Gain all you can, without hurting either yourself or your neighbour, in soul or body, by applying hereto with unintermitted diligence, and with all the understanding which God has given you;—save all you can, by cutting off every expense which serves only to indulge foolish desire; to gratify either the desire of flesh, the desire of the eye, or the pride of life; waste nothing, living or dying, on sin or folly, whether for yourself or your children;—and then, give all you can, or, in other words, give all you have to God. Do not stint yourself, like a Jew rather than a Christian, to this or that proportion. "Render unto God," not a tenth, not a third, not half, but all that is God's, be it more or less; by employing all on yourself, your household, the household of faith, and all mankind, in such a manner, that you may give a good account of your stewardship when ye can be no longer stewards; in such a manner as the oracles of God direct, both by general and particular precepts; in such a manner, that whatever ye do may be "a sacrifice of a sweet-smelling savour to God," and that every act may be rewarded in that day when the Lord cometh with all his saints.

7. Brethren, can we be either wise or faithful stewards unless we thus manage our Lord's goods? We cannot, as not only the oracles of God, but our own conscience beareth witness. Then why should we delay? Why should we confer any longer with flesh and blood, or men of the world? Our kingdom, our wisdom is not of this world:

Heathen custom is nothing to us. We follow no men any farther than they are followers of Christ. Hear ye him. Yea, to-day, while it is called to-day, hear and obey his voice! At this hour, and from this hour, do his will: Fulfil his word, in this and in all things! I entreat you, in the name of the Lord Jesus, act up to the dignity of your calling! No more sloth! Whatsoever your hand findeth to do, do it with your might! No more waste! Cut off every expense which fashion, caprice, or flesh and blood demand! No more covetousness! But employ whatever God has entrusted you with, in doing good, all possible good, in every possible kind and degree to the household of faith, to all men! This is no small part of "the wisdom of the just." Give all ye have, as well as all ye are, a spiritual sacrifice to Him who withheld not from you his Son, his only Son: So "laying up in store for yourselves a good foundation against the time to come, that ye may attain eternal life"!

Notes

Prequel

1. Sondra E. Wheeler, *Wealth and Peril as Obligation* (Grand Rapids: Eerdmans, 1995), 122.
2. Ibid., 124–25.
3. Ibid., 125.
4. See the full treatment of the wisdom prosperity texts, 29–42.
5. Wheeler, *Wealth and Peril*, 128–29.
6. Ibid., 130.

Chapter 1 "In the Beginning God Created . . ."

1. Wendell Berry, "Sabbaths 2005," XII. This poem has not been published in a formal public collection, except apparently in a chapbook, or self-published volume, and then made available for general public use online (http://shenandoah.wlu.edu/BerryPoems.pdf).
2. Quoting Paul Johnson, *A History of the Jews* (New York: HarperCollins, 1987), 172–73.
3. "Usury," Wikipedia, http://en.wikipedia.org/wiki/Usury (accessed June 13, 2009).
4. See my discussion on this subject in Ben Witherington III, *The Letters to Philemon, the Colossians, and the Ephesians* (Grand Rapids: Eerdmans, 2007), 87–90.
5. There is a fine book by Brian Rosner entitled *Greed as Idolatry: The Origin and Meaning of a Pauline Metaphor* (Grand Rapids: Eerdmans, 2007), which extends the discussion of this idea into the New Testament.

Chapter 2 A King's Ransom

1. For a much fuller discussion of this whole matter see Ben Witherington III, *Jesus the Sage*, rev. ed. (Minneapolis: Fortress, 2000), 3–116.

2. Robert Gordis, "The Social Background of Wisdom Literature," *HUCA* 18 (1944): 77–118, here 81–82.

3. James Crenshaw, *Old Testament Wisdom: An Introduction* (Louisville: Westminster/John Knox, 1981), 67.

4. Sometimes associated with the Word of Faith theology.

5. For a detailed discussion of the origins and provenance of Ecclesiastes see Witherington, *Jesus the Sage,* 52–54.

Chapter 3 Money in the Bartering World of Jesus

1. D. E. Oakman, "Economics of Palestine," in *Dictionary of New Testament Background*, ed. Craig A. Evans and Stanley E. Porter (Downers Grove, IL: InterVarsity, 2000), 303–8, here 303. In this section of the chapter, I basically follow Oakman's lead, as he is the real expert in these matters.

2. Ibid., 304.

3. Ibid.

4. Ekkehard W. Stegemann and Wolfgang Stegemann, *The Jesus Movement: A Social History of Its First Century* (Minneapolis: Fortress, 1999), 100.

5. See below, 94–99.

6. See Josephus, *Jewish War* 3.41–45.

7. Stegemann and Stegemann, *Jesus Movement*, 105.

8. It needs to be stressed, however, that the economic situation became more complicated when the land was parceled out to Herod's three sons, and in effect became three rather independent regions. There was, for example, a problem caused by each of these rulers minting their own coins, and the question arose about equivalencies.

9. See Stegemann and Stegemann, *Jesus Movement*, 112.

10. Ibid.

11. *m. Shevi'it* 10:2–4.

12. This tax fell into abeyance when the temple was destroyed in AD 70, only to be replaced by the much more repugnant *fiscus Judaicus*, or Roman tax imposed on conquered peoples to show that their complete defeat went to the temple of Jupiter Optimus Maximus. This tax was so egregious in part because it was imposed on every Jew between the ages of three and sixty-two years old; see Stegemann and Stegemann, *Jesus Movement*, 120.

13. Philo, *On the Special Laws* 1.78.

14. Josephus, *The Life* 63.

15. For more on Jewish coins see Théodore Reinach, *Jewish Coins,* trans. Mary Hill (Chicago: Argonaut, 1966).

16. On this matter see Ben Witherington III, *Women in the Ministry of Jesus* (Cambridge: Cambridge University Press, 1984).

Chapter 4 Jesus and the Treasure Hunt

1. See Ben Witherington III, *Women in the Ministry of Jesus* (Cambridge: Cambridge University Press,1984).

2. For a more detailed discussion of this story, see Ben Witherington III, *The Christology of Jesus* (Minneapolis: Fortress, 1990), 101–4.

3. See the helpful discussion in L. Joseph Kreitzer, *Striking New Images: Roman Imperial Coinage and the New Testament* (Sheffield: Sheffield Academic Press, 1996).
4. See Josephus, *Jewish Antiquities* 3.8.2, and *m. Sheqalim* 1:1.
5. See 4Q Ordinances.
6. See, for example, Rom. 13, and possibly 1 Pet. 2:3–17.
7. An exhortation not found in the Matthean parallel. It presupposes the audience has resources to sell and worth selling.
8. As in *m. Pe'ah* 1:1; *b. Shabbat* 156b; *b. Rosh HaShanah* 16b.
9. Craig Evans, *Luke*, NIBC (Peabody, MA: Hendrickson, 1990), 197.
10. Luke Timothy Johnson, *The Gospel of Luke*, SP (Collegeville, MN: Liturgical, 1991), 199.
11. See John Duncan M. Derrett, *Law in the New Testament* (London: Darton, Longman and Todd, 1970), 48–77.
12. Joseph A. Fitzmyer, *The Gospel according to Luke X–XXIV*, AB 28A (New York: Doubleday, 1985), 1097–113.
13. Evans, *Luke*, 239.
14. See the discussion about Wisdom literature, 29–42.
15. Q is the abbreviation for a collection of mostly sayings found in and used only by Matthew and Luke, but not Mark (or John).
16. John Nolland, *Luke 9.21–18.34*, WBC 35b (Waco, TX: Word, 1993), 807.
17. See Josephus, *Jewish Antiquities* 4.238.
18. See Sirach on this matter.
19. On all of this one should read the helpful narrative re-creation by Gerd Theissen, *The Shadow of the Galilean: The Quest for the Historical Jesus in Narrative Form* (Minneapolis: Fortress, 2007).
20. See below, 127–128.
21. Here Joseph Fitzmyer (*The Gospel according to Luke I–IX*, AB 28 [New York: Doubleday, 1981], 632) is right to point out that "you" is likely introduced into these beatitudes and woes by Luke, not only because Luke has a preference for the second person plural but also because earlier sapiential sayings of this sort regularly used the third person. See the following note as well.
22. So we have four descriptions of what happens to a particular person whether blessed or blighted. See Frederick W. Danker, *Jesus and the New Age according to St. Luke: A Commentary on the Third Gospel* (St. Louis: Clayton, 1972), 142.
23. See Josephus, *Jewish Antiquities* 20.180–81, 205–7. On all of this see Ben Witherington III, *The Gospel of Mark* (Grand Rapids: Eerdmans, 2001), 334–36.
24. See discussion above, 53.

Chapter 5 James's Rich Wisdom

1. For a lengthy treatment of the material reviewed here in cursory fashion, see Ben Witherington III, *Letters and Homilies for Jewish Christians: Hebrews, James, Jude* (Downers Grove, IL: InterVarsity, 2007).
2. See Sir. 7:6–7 on the former and Sir. 35:10–18 on the latter.
3. One could actually argue that, since Lev. 19:15 on the love of neighbor is placed near this text, James is doing an exposition of this whole portion of Leviticus at least at the outset of his discourse here. See Luke Timothy Johnson, "The Use of Leviticus 19 in the Letter of James," *JBL* 101 (1982): 391–401.

4. Compare *Didache* 16.2; Ignatius, *To Polycarp* 4.2.

5. This is not necessarily the case. Having spent a fair bit of time in mosques and churches in the Middle East, I know that the majority of the people are poorly clad and smell, but this does not mean they are beggars. It has to do with the climate.

6. This is the suggestion of Edward A. Judge in *New Documents Illustrating Early Christianity*, vol. 1, *A Review of the Greek Inscriptions and Papyri Published in 1976*, ed. G. H. R. Horsley (Sydney: Macquarrie University Press, 1981), 111. On this same page we also have the translation of inscriptional evidence from SEG 1683 which says in part: "The synagogue of the Jews honored Tation, daughter of Straton, . . . with a gold crown and a seat of honor." This was because Tation paid for the provision of certain parts of the synagogue. It is thus possible we have a similar sort of scene being described here by James.

7. Luke Timothy Johnson, *Letter of James*, AB 37A (New York: Doubleday, 1995), 222–23.

8. Cf. Pss. 12:4; 24:16; 32:13; 68:17, all in the Septuagint.

9. At the same time, it is not implied that the poor had more material possessions or more abundant faith than the rich. No comparison is made at all. It is quite clear that the kingdom mentioned here is viewed as future: it is what God has promised to those who love him, a promise not yet fulfilled.

10. Elsa Tamez, *The Scandalous Message of James: Faith without Works Is Dead* (New York: Crossroad, 1990), 44–45.

11. Alfred Plummer, *St. James and St. Jude* (London: Hodder and Stoughton, 1891), 125. Italics mine.

12. Johnson, *Letter of James*, 239.

13. Peter Davids, *The Epistle of James: A Commentary on the Greek Text*, NIGTC (Grand Rapids: Eerdmans, 1982), 122.

14. J. B. Mayor, *The Epistle of St. James*, 3rd ed. (London: MacMillan, 1910), 154. Greek words have been transliterated.

15. See Jdt. 16:17.

16. Johnson, *Letter of James*, 301. The remark becomes highly sarcastic or ironic in this case.

17. William W. Brosend, *James and Jude*, NCBC (Cambridge: Cambridge University Press, 2004), 134.

Chapter 6 Wealth and Poverty In Luke-Acts

1. On this see Ben Witherington III, "Appendix 2: Salvation and Health in Christian Antiquity," in *The Acts of the Apostles* (Grand Rapids: Eerdmans, 1998), 821–43.

2. See the discussion in Ben Witherington III, *Women in the Earliest Churches* (Cambridge: Cambridge University Press, 1988), 128–29.

3. In regard to the form of the text given here in the Greek New Testament in Luke 4:18–19 it is clearly in agreement with the Septuagint rather than the Hebrew text.

4. See above, 50.

5. Most scholars have concluded, probably rightly, that Jesus was executed in AD 30. To judge from the Fourth Gospel, Jesus's ministry certainly lasted more than a single year, and so it is plausible that Jesus did cite this text at a propitious moment in the Jewish calendar. See I. Howard Marshall, *The Gospel of Luke: A Commentary*

on the Greek Text, NIGTC (Grand Rapids: Eerdmans; Exeter: Paternoster, 1978), 184–85.

6. See the detailed discussion in Ben Witherington III, *Jesus the Seer* (Peabody, MA: Hendrickson, 1999).

7. John Nolland, *Luke 1–9:20*, WBC 35a (Waco, TX: Word, 1989), 201.

8. See *b. Qiddushin* 72a–b; the spot of highest honor in heaven from the Jewish viewpoint.

9. Scholars have sometimes compared Acts 2:42–47 to the practices at Qumran with some profit (see 1QS V, 1–3; IX, 3–11; CD IX, 1–15), but there the motivation was the demands for ritual purity and the avoidance of sin, not an ideal of true brotherhood or friendship.

10. It is interesting that this description does seem to mirror Greco-Roman notions about how true friends share all things in common (see Plato, *Republic* 449C; *Critias* 110C–D; Aristotle, *Nicomachean Ethics* 1168B; Philo, *On the Life of Abraham* 235). Perhaps Theophilus was meant to relate such notions, with which he would be familiar, to this exposition suggesting that Christians actually practiced ideal friendship, perhaps also prompting him to be a patron of a Christian community.

11. On all of this and for much more detailed discussion, see Witherington, *Acts of the Apostles*, 204–9. Here again this may be a prompt for Theophilus's benefit.

12. See discussion of the widow's mite, 53.

13. Justo González, *Faith and Wealth: A History of Early Christian Ideas on the Origin, Significance, and Use of Money* (Eugene, OR: Wipf and Stock, 1990), 82.

Chapter 7 Paul—On Work, Remuneration, and the Love of Money

1. The reader wanting details and interaction with the secondary literature should look at Ben Witherington III, *Grace in Galatia* (Grand Rapids: Eerdmans, 1998), 417–38.

2. J. G. Strelan, "Burden-Bearing and the Law of Christ: A Re-examination of Galatians 6.2," *JBL* 94 (1975): 266–76.

3. See John Bligh, *Galatians: A Study of Paul's Epistle* (London: St. Paul, 1969), 486.

4. Larry W. Hurtado, "The Jerusalem Collection and the Book of Galatians," *JSNT* 5 (1979): 46–62. This last suggestion can perhaps build on Gal. 2:10, since it seems strange that Paul would simply drop the matter with the passing reference in 2:10. Another example of the fruitfulness of Strelan's argument can be seen when one pays attention to the fact that 6:3 is connected to 6:2 by means of a *gar* (for). Unless the term is purely superfluous, then one must posit some connection between "bear one another's burdens" and "if anyone thinks he is something. . . ." Strelan plausibly suggests that Paul has in mind a person who balks at the thought of having to share a common financial burden with persons of lower social status, because of that person's sense of self-importance. "No matter how important a man is or thinks he is, he is not relieved of the obligation to take a responsible share of the work in and for the Lord" (Strelan, "Burden-Bearing," 271). Or again a connection can be seen between 6:5 and 6:6, with the latter being a qualification of the former. Christians should carry their own weight financially, but when someone gives a great deal of their own time to the task of teaching fellow Christians, there is an obligation to

support such a person. This builds on the notion that Paul has in mind a saying of Jesus in 6:6 (cf. below).

5. See Sir. 13:2; compare Neh. 5:18.

6. Richard B. Hays, "Christology and Ethics in Galatians: The Law of Christ," *CBQ* 49 (1987): 268–90, here 280. He rightly points to the similar sort of discussion in Rom. 15:1–9.

7. I have addressed the issue of what was called in antiquity inoffensive self-praise and how Paul deals with these conventions in Ben Witherington III, *Conflict and Community in Corinth* (Grand Rapids: Eerdmans, 1994), 432–37. The key points for this discussion are: (1) self-praise was a primary characteristic of popular teachers of the day, both rhetors and philosophers; (2) it was acceptable to refer to one's own real accomplishments, but it was arrogant to claim more than was the case (see Cicero, *On Invention* 1.16.22); (3) the extent to which these conventions were followed and considered important throughout the empire is shown by the treatise of Paul's near contemporary, Plutarch, entitled *On Inoffensive Self-Praise*; (4) Paul tends to use these conventions but in a highly ironic way, as is shown in 2 Corinthians 10–13. See the discussion in Edward A. Judge, "Paul's Boasting in Relation to Contemporary Professional Practice," *ABR* 16 (1968): 37–48; and in C. Forbes, "Comparison, Self-Praise and Irony," *NTS* 32 (1986): 1–30.

8. Cf. Xenophon, *Memorabilia* 3.13.6.

9. James D. G. Dunn, *The Epistle to the Galatians* (Peabody, MA: Hendrickson, 1993), 326.

10. Notice that it is "the word" that the teachers teach, here referring to the Christian message, presumably the message of salvation focusing on the story of Jesus Christ.

11. Cf. Aristotle, *Rhetoric* 3.3.4; Plato, *Phaedrus* 260D; Job 4:8; Prov. 22:8; Jer. 12:13; Sir. 7:3; *Testament of Levi* 13.6.

12. This issue is addressed in some detail in 1 Thess. 4:11 ("mind your own business, work with your own hands . . . so that you will not be dependent on anybody") and 5:14 ("warn the idle"); and 2 Thess. 3:10 ("let those who will not work, not eat").

13. See also *Genesis Rabbah* 2.2 on Gen. 1:2.

14. Sometimes, like musicians in a subway station in London, orators would speak in a forum or agora ex tempore, but with expectation that appreciative observers would shell out some coins. This was not patronage per se, nor was it patronage when one went to the Odeon to hear an orator on which occasion one would buy tickets.

15. For more on all the Corinthian material, see Witherington, *Conflict and Community*.

16. Cf. Seneca, *Epistle* 108; Epictetus, *Dissertations* 3.13.7; Marcus Aurelius, *To Himself* 6.16; Josephus, *Jewish Antiquities* 12.294; 2 Macc. 5:15; 4 Macc. 6:28.

17. There is an interesting inscription cited in *New Documents Illustrating Early Christianity* (vol. 4, *A Review of the Greek Inscriptions and Papyri Published in 1979*, ed. G. H. R. Horsley [Sydney: Macquarrie University Press, 1987], 169) from Ephesus in AD 44, where the proconsul Paullus Fabius Persicus censures those who sought to make *porismos* (only here at 1 Tim. 6:5–6 in the New Testament), personal financial gain, through using religion, in particular through selling priesthoods as though at auction. Clearly, religion for personal profit was a known problem and evil in Ephesus in this era.

18. See also Wis. 7:6; Seneca, *Epistle* 102.25.

19. Cf. Aristotle, *Politics* 1336A on the former meaning and Aristotle, *Metaphysics* 1043A on the latter. This saying too is a maxim (cf. Sir. 29:21; Plutarch, *Dinner of Seven Sages* 12).

20. Craig Blomberg, *Neither Poverty nor Riches* (Downers Grove, IL: InterVarsity, 1999), 230.

21. Cf. for example the RSV, which makes the mistake of putting the definite article before "root" so that it reads "money is *the* root . . ."

22. Cf. Philo, *On the Decalogue* 5, 173; *On the Special Laws* 1.121; *On the Contemplative Life* 39.

23. Cited in Diogenes Laertius, *Lives of Eminent Philosophers* 6.50; cf. on the idea Stobaeus, *Eclogues* 3; *Testament of Judah* 19.1; Didorous Siculus, 21.1; Philo, *On the Special Laws* 4.65.

24. Dio Chrysostom, *Oration* 54.1.

25. Throughout this section of 1 Timothy it is necessary always to keep in mind the way the rhetoric of Wisdom literature works. It provides general principles or truths often in colorful or memorable and figurative wording, and it presupposes a rather specific religious and social context in which a particular saying holds true. Sometimes it deliberately involves rhetorical hyperbole, for instance in the maxim above, which could even be translated "the love of money is a root of every kind of evil." If this is the correct translation, and it may well be in view of the emphatic position of the word *root*, then it is in order to point out that the rhetorical function of hyperbole is to dramatically emphasize something, drawing attention to it and trying to inculcate a strong sympathetic response in the audience, in this case to urge them to avoid avarice. Such polemical maxims are not meant to be taken absolutely literally.

26. See also 2 Macc. 14:34; Philo, *Against Flaccus* 121; *On the Virtues* 57; Josephus, *Jewish Antiquities* 4.40.

27. Joscphus, *Jewish War* 5.380.

28. Seneca, *Natural Questions* 3, preface 14; cf. Athenagoras, *Embassy for the Christians* 13.2; *1 Clement* 29.1.

29. Cf. Josephus, *Jewish War* 2.8.4.

30. Josephus, *Jewish Antiquities* 6.262; Philo, *On the Embassy to Gaius* 352.

31. Philo, *On the Life of Moses* 2.234; *On the Contemplative Life* 33; *Against Flaccus* 89.

32. John Chrysostom, *Homily 8 on 1 Timothy*.

33. James B. Hurley, *Man and Woman in Biblical Perspective* (Downers Grove, IL: InterVarsity, 1981), 199. There is extensive material along these lines in his doctoral dissertation, *Man and Woman in Corinth* (PhD diss., Cambridge University, 1973). See John Percy V. D. Balsdon, *Roman Women* (London: Bodley Head, 1962).

34. *Testament of Reuben* 5.5; cf. Juvenal, *Satire* 6; Plutarch, *Moralia* 141E.

35. See, e.g., Aristotle, *Nicomachean Ethics* 3.10–12.

Chapter 8   John of Patmos and a News Flash for the Merchants and Mr. 666

1. See Tacitus, *Annals* 4.55–56.

2. J. Nelson Kraybill, *Imperial Cult and Commerce in John's Apocalypse* (Sheffield: Sheffield Academic Press, 1996).

3. See the detailed discussion in Ben Witherington III, *Revelation* (Cambridge: Cambridge University Press, 2003).

4. Not just in American life. One sees such examples in places like Germany and elsewhere in Europe and Asia. For example, there are millions of Turks in Germany who work as the underclass doing the blue-collar jobs the Germans mostly will not do at this juncture for that sort of low pay. But when some raise the question of Turks becoming German citizens in larger numbers, there is all too predictably an outcry.

Chapter 9 Towards a New Testament Theology of Money, Stewardship, and Giving

1. Sondra E. Wheeler, *Wealth and Peril as Obligation* (Grand Rapids: Eerdmans, 1995), 122.

2. See Ibid., 129–32.

3. Ibid., 133–34.

4. Ibid., 139–40.

5. Craig Blomberg, *Neither Poverty nor Riches* (Downers Grove, IL: InterVarsity, 1999), 244.

6. Ibid., 245.

7. Aristotle, *Nicomachean Ethics* 4.1.19.

8. See Ben Witherington III, *Philemon, Colossians, and Ephesians* (Grand Rapids: Eerdmans, 2007).

9. I will say much more about this in the sequel to this book on a Christian view of work and rest and play.

Appendix 1: Ten Christian Myths about Money

1. I am working on a forthcoming book about what the Bible has to say about work.